National Defense Research Institute

T0167400

# SOLDIERS

# FOR

# PEACE

*Critical Operational Issues*

BRUCE R. PIRNIE

WILLIAM E. SIMONS

Prepared for the
Office of the Secretary of Defense

# RAND

As a power with global interests, the United States has a strong concern for successful peace operations. Seldom if ever will its interests be well served by failures, especially widely publicized and expensive failures that tend to discredit the United Nations. This report presents the results of Phase Two of "Guidelines for U.S. Involvement in Peace Operations," a two-phase project sponsored by the Office of the Assistant Secretary of Defense (Strategy and Requirements). (The results of Phase One are presented in Bruce R. Pirnie and William E. Simons, *Soldiers for Peace: An Operational Typology*, RAND, Santa Monica, Calif., MR-582-OSD, 1996.) It identifies critical issues that must be resolved to ensure reasonable prospects for a peace operation's success. It builds upon and further develops *The Clinton Administration's Policy on Reforming Multilateral Peace Operations* (U.S. State Department, Washington, D.C., Publication 10161, May 1994), where most of those issues are raised. The report illustrates issues with examples drawn from past and current operations. These examples were chosen to enliven the discourse and to emphasize insights gained through painful experience.

The purpose of this report is to assist U.S. decisionmakers by providing a checklist that can be used to plan a new operation or to evaluate an operation already in progress. As a founder of the United Nations, permanent member of the Security Council, and leading power in the world, the United States has a primary responsibility to ensure that peace operations are well conducted. But the checklist developed in this report could also be used by other member states associated with peace operations, by United Nations staff, and by private associations or individuals concerned with the subject of peace operations.

Research for this project was completed in spring 1995. The authors have generally retained this information-cutoff date, except for operations in the former Yugoslavia. The collapse of the exclusion zone around Sarajevo in June, the fall of Srebrenica in July, the invasion of Krajina in August, and the successful NATO bombing campaign in September are so well-known and instructive that the authors were impelled to include them.

This research was performed within the International Security and Defense Policy Center of RAND's National Defense Research Institute, a federally funded research and development center sponsored by the Office of the Secretary of Defense, the Joint Staff, and the defense agencies. Comments and inquiries are welcome and should be addressed to the authors.

# CONTENTS

Preface . . . . . . . . . . . . . . . . . . . . . . . . . . . . . . . . . . . . . . . . . .   iii

Figures . . . . . . . . . . . . . . . . . . . . . . . . . . . . . . . . . . . . . . . . . .   ix

Summary . . . . . . . . . . . . . . . . . . . . . . . . . . . . . . . . . . . . . . . .   xi

Acknowledgments . . . . . . . . . . . . . . . . . . . . . . . . . . . . . . . . . . .   xxv

Acronyms and Abbreviations . . . . . . . . . . . . . . . . . . . . . . . . . .   xxvii

Chapter One
    INTRODUCTION . . . . . . . . . . . . . . . . . . . . . . . . . . . . . . .   1
    What Are Peace Operations? . . . . . . . . . . . . . . . . . . . . . . .   2
        Consent and Impartiality . . . . . . . . . . . . . . . . . . . . . . .   2
        Chapter VI and Chapter VII . . . . . . . . . . . . . . . . . . . .   3
        Spectrum of Peace Operations . . . . . . . . . . . . . . . . . . .   4
        Intervention in Internal Crises . . . . . . . . . . . . . . . . . . .   5
    Role of the United States . . . . . . . . . . . . . . . . . . . . . . . . .   6
    Checklist of Critical Issues . . . . . . . . . . . . . . . . . . . . . . . .   6

Chapter Two
    COMMENTARY ON *ADMINISTRATION'S POLICY* . . . . . .   11
    Applying *Administration's Policy* . . . . . . . . . . . . . . . . . .   11
    Should the United States Vote Affirmatively? . . . . . . . . . .   12
        U.S. Interests and Community of Interest . . . . . . . . . . .   12
        Threat to Peace and Security . . . . . . . . . . . . . . . . . . . .   14
        Spectrum of Peace Operations . . . . . . . . . . . . . . . . . . .   19
        Chapter VI Peace-Keeping . . . . . . . . . . . . . . . . . . . . . .   20
        Chapter VII Peace Enforcement . . . . . . . . . . . . . . . . . .   20
        Means and Mandate . . . . . . . . . . . . . . . . . . . . . . . . . .   21

Is Inaction Unacceptable? ...................... 21
Anticipated Duration ........................... 22
Should the United States Participate? ................ 22
Issues Concerning U.S. Participation .............. 23
Summary of Issues Concerning U.S. Participation ..... 25

Chapter Three
NATURE OF THE CONFLICT ..................... 27
Stage of the Conflict ........................... 27
Prevalence of Unconventional Warfare .............. 28
Irreconcilable Aims and Animosity ................. 29
Degree of Control over Combatants ................. 30
Risk to Personnel ............................. 31

Chapter Four
CONSENT OF THE PARTIES ..................... 33
Peace-Keeping ................................ 33
Observation to Facilitate Agreements .............. 33
Observation to Deter Violations .................. 37
Interposition to Facilitate Agreements ............. 37
Interposition to Deter Violations ................. 40
More-Ambitious Operations ...................... 41
Transition ................................. 41
Security for Humanitarian Aid ................... 44
Peace Enforcement ........................... 47

Chapter Five
MANDATE ................................... 51
Peace-Keeping ................................ 52
Observation ................................ 52
Interposition ............................... 53
More-Ambitious Operations ...................... 56
Transition ................................. 56
Security for Humanitarian Aid ................... 60
Peace Enforcement ........................... 64

Chapter Six
CHARACTER OF THE PEACE FORCE ............... 69
Control over Combat Operations ................... 70
Peace-Keeping ................................ 73
Observation ................................ 73
Interposition ............................... 75

More-Ambitious Operations ...................... 77
   Transition ................................... 78
   Security for Humanitarian Aid .................. 81
   Peace Enforcement ........................... 84

Chapter Seven
PHYSICAL ENVIRONMENT ...................... 91
Peace-Keeping ............................... 91
   Observation.................................. 91
   Interposition ................................. 92
More-Ambitious Operations ...................... 93
   Transition ................................... 93
   Security for Humanitarian Aid .................. 94
   Peace Enforcement ........................... 95

Chapter Eight
EXTENT OF INTERNATIONAL SUPPORT ............ 97
Peace-Keeping ............................... 98
   Observation.................................. 98
   Interposition ................................. 99
More-Ambitious Operations ...................... 101
   Transition ................................... 101
   Security for Humanitarian Aid .................. 104
   Peace Enforcement ........................... 105

Chapter Nine
CONCLUSION ................................ 109
Judging the Stage of Conflict ..................... 109
Holding Parties to Their Word .................... 110
Ensuring That Mandates Are Feasible .............. 111
Making Operations Consonant with Political Will ....... 112

Appendix
A.  TERMS USED IN THIS REPORT ................... 113
B.  *AGENDA FOR PEACE*........................... 119
C.  STANDARDS FOR U.S. INVOLVEMENT .............. 125

Select Bibliography ................................ 129

# FIGURES

S.1. Spectrum of Peace Operations . . . . . . . . . . . . . . . . .    xiii
1.1. Spectrum of Peace Operations . . . . . . . . . . . . . . . .     4
2.1. Issues Concerning U.S. Participation . . . . . . . . . . . .    25
6.1. Options for Control of Forces . . . . . . . . . . . . . . . . .   71
B.1. Typology of Peace Operations in *Agenda for Peace—1992* . . . . . . . . . . . . . . . . . . . . . . . . . . . .   122

# SUMMARY

In spring 1994, the United States published *The Clinton Administration's Policy on Reforming Multilateral Peace Operations* (U.S. State Department, Washington, D.C., Publication 10161, May 1994). This document offered a starting point for operational reform but needed further development. This report develops *Administration's Policy* by exploring issues raised in that document and additional issues implied by the subject. It relates U.S. decisions on voting affirmatively and participation to the fundamental problem of ensuring reasonable prospects for success, especially in peace operations conducted under Chapter VII of the United Nations Charter. It provides a comprehensive set of critical issues and illustrates these issues with examples chosen from peace operations conducted during the past five decades.

## WHAT ARE PEACE OPERATIONS?

Peace operations are not described in the Charter of the United Nations. They seem to fall somewhere between Chapter VI (Pacific Settlement of Disputes) and Chapter VII (Action with Respect to Threats to the Peace, Breaches of the Peace, and Acts of Aggression). The Security Council has usually invoked Chapter VI, implying that lethal force will be used only in self-defense while accomplishing the mandate. But in some cases, the Security Council has invoked Chapter VII, implying that lethal force will be used against a recalcitrant party. Two criteria bound the domain of peace operations:

consent of the parties and impartiality[1] on the part of the Security Council.

## Consent

*Consent* is the evident willingness of parties to cooperate in accomplishing the mandate. Parties may subsequently withdraw their consent, but to date no peace operation has begun without initial consent from the parties.

## Impartiality

*Impartiality* means that the Security Council does not take sides, because it judges that all parties share responsibility for a conflict. It does not imply that every action taken by the Security Council during a peace operation will affect all parties equally. Indeed, even the least intrusive peace operation is unlikely to affect all parties equally.

## SPECTRUM OF PEACE OPERATIONS

*Administration's Policy* mentions a spectrum of peace operations but does not offer a definition of that spectrum, other than to distinguish between traditional peace-keeping under Chapter VI and peace enforcement under Chapter VII. A complete typology is presented in Bruce R. Pirnie and William E. Simons, *Soldiers for Peace: An Operational Typology*, RAND, Santa Monica, Calif., MR-582-OSD, 1996, the companion piece to this report. This typology, developed from an operational perspective, provides a foundation for examining and resolving critical issues. It includes five types of peace operations: observation (at the low end in cost and risk), interposition, transition, security for humanitarian aid, and peace enforcement (at the high end). Figure S.1 displays these types in a spectrum.

---

[1]See Appendix A for definitions of terms used in this report.

RAND*MR583-S.1*

| | Peace Operations | | | | | | |
|---|---|---|---|---|---|---|---|
| | Peace-Keeping | | | | More-Ambitious Operations | | |
| | Observation | | Interposition | | Transition | Security for Humanitarian Aid | Peace Enforcement |
| | Facilitate agreement | Deter violations | Facilitate agreement | Deter violations | | | |
| Chapter of the U.N. Charter | Chapter VI (self-defense) | | | | Chapter VI (self-defense) / Chapter VII (potential enforcement) | Chapter VII (secure aid) | Chapter VII (enforce will of UNSC) |
| Consent Required from the Parties | Allow access to observers | | Acquiesce in impartial control of a buffer zone | | Cooperate in achieving new condition and status of a country | Allow provision of aid | None: occurs when party *withdraws* consent |
| Typical Mandate | Observe compliance with agreements; report violations; mediate among parties | Plus respond forcefully to violations | Create buffer zones; control entry into buffer zones; monitor arms limitations | Plus respond forcefully to violations | Provide secure conditions; oversee demobilization, demilitarization, arms limitations; provide security for electoral activities; facilitate reconstruction; cooperate closely with civilian component and NGOs | Provide security for humanitarian aid | Coerce recalcitrant parties into complying with UNSC resolutions and parties' agreements |

← Chapter VI → | ← Chapter VII →

**Figure S.1—Spectrum of Peace Operations**

## Peace-Keeping

*Peace-keeping* includes observation and interposition conducted under Chapter VI. *Observation* involves monitoring compliance with agreements, reporting violations, and mediating resolution of violations. *Interposition* requires the peace force to control a buffer zone between the opposing parties. Peace-keeping has usually been intended to facilitate agreements, leaving the onus for keeping their agreements on the parties. But in two cases (Macedonia, Kuwait), peace-keeping is intended to deter violations ("preventive deployment"), implying that the Security Council would respond forcefully if violations occurred.

## More-Ambitious Operations

*More-ambitious operations,* especially prevalent since the end of the Cold War, include transition, security for humanitarian aid, and peace enforcement. *Transition operations* are intended to change the condition and status of a country—for example, by reconciling warring parties within a new governmental structure. More narrowly, the Council may decide to *secure humanitarian aid,* thus alleviating suffering caused by conflict. *Peace enforcement* has ensued when parties withdrew consent during operations conducted under Chapter VII and the Security Council attempted to coerce them.

## THE SPECTRUM IS DISCONTINUOUS

The spectrum of peace operations is not a smooth continuum. On the contrary, it is discontinuous, meaning that the Security Council should not attempt to move across the spectrum without facing the implications of certain decisions: whether to attempt "preventive deployment," invoke Chapter VII, and initiate peace enforcement.

### "Preventive Deployment"

When the Security Council decides to use "preventive deployment," it indicates determination to respond promptly and forcefully if violations occur. Therefore, the Security Council or its agents must prepare such a response or risk loss of prestige if challenged.

### Invoking Chapter VII

Invoking Chapter VII implies willingness to coerce parties that violate their agreements or resolutions of the Security Council. Therefore, the Security Council should select a capable agent and should be certain that member states will provide adequate forces. Absent these preparations, recalcitrant parties might feel encouraged to defy the Council.

### Peace Enforcement

When the Security Council decides to coerce a recalcitrant party, it crosses a Rubicon between noncoercive operations with continuous consent and coercive operations to impose the will of the Council. The peace force ceases to be a noncombatant, relying on restraint of the parties for its security, and becomes a combatant, relying on its own combat power for security. An attempt to mingle such radically dissimilar roles might cause the operation to degenerate into confused half-measures, as occurred in Somalia and Bosnia-Herzegovina.

## CHECKLIST OF CRITICAL ISSUES

Critical issues should be resolved whenever a peace operation is contemplated or is evaluated while in progress. These issues are subsumed under six headings:  nature of the conflict, consent of the parties, mandate, character of the peace force, physical environment, and extent of international support.

### Nature of the Conflict

How amenable is the conflict to peace operations? The following five aspects should be considered when answering this question:

**Stage of the Conflict.**  Once fighting has broken out, a conflict may not be amenable to peace operations until culmination or stalemate is reached. *Culmination* is reached when a stronger party has attained important aims and cannot attain more aims through force. *Stalemate* occurs when parties countervail so that no party is likely to attain its aims through force. Culmination is usually more propitious for peace operations than stalemate, because parties are reluctant to concede that stalemate cannot be overcome.

**Prevalence of Unconventional Warfare.** *Unconventional warfare* involves irregular forces employing raiding tactics. There may be no lines of confrontation, or combatants may operate extensively behind the lines.  The distinction between combatants and noncombatants may be obscured. Under such circumstances, peace operations may be severely hampered or made unworkable. The techniques of traditional peace-keeping are particularly ill-suited to handling unconventional warfare.

**Irreconcilable Aims and Animosity.** Parties have opposing aims that they seek to realize through force or threat of force. As an outcome of conflict, they may abandon those aims or modify them until they can be reconciled, or they may continue to have irreconcilable aims. Irreconcilable aims imply that the conflict may break out again later, even if the peace operation is successful. The tenacity with which parties hold to particular aims may be increased by animosity that has built up during the conflict. When that animosity becomes visceral, it makes some types of peace operation unworkable, especially those that require the parties to cooperate with each other.

**Degree of Control over Combatants.** So long as the parties maintain their consent, conflict is more amenable to peace operations when the parties exert strong control over combatants. Lack of control hampers peace operations by blurring responsibility for disruptive actions. Implicit in peace-keeping is an expectation that the parties will implement their agreements, based on a presumption that the parties control their adherents. Absent such control, there may be little point in monitoring activity for which no party will accept responsibility.

**Risk to Personnel in the Peace Force.** All peace operations involve some risk to personnel, both military and civilian. The acceptable level of risk varies according to the type of operation and the level of support from member states. Operations under Chapter VI normally entail low risk to personnel; indeed, high risk would invalidate the very concept. By contrast, participating states should anticipate casualties during operations under Chapter VII.

## Consent of the Parties

How willing are the parties to help accomplish the mandate? Willingness is manifested through formal or actual consent. *Formal* consent is manifested in statements, declarations, accords, agreements, and treaties. *Actual* consent becomes apparent from the behavior of the parties in the course of a peace operation. Therefore, the answer cannot be known with certainty until the operation is under way.

Consent is central to all peace operations, including peace enforcement, which may be undertaken when consent is lost. To understand how consent affects an operation, the Security Council needs to consider how much consent is required, its current status, the prospects for maintaining it, and, finally, how the Council intends to respond if parties withdraw their consent. When parties refuse to cooperate, the Security Council might try to coerce them through sanctions or by authorizing peace enforcement. Alternatively, the Council might promote negotiations among the parties, change to a less intrusive mandate, or terminate the operation.

## Mandate

Are the purpose and scope of the operation well defined? Mandates define what is expected from the parties and what the peace force is expected to accomplish—in other words, its mission. Of all the critical issues, those concerning mandates are the most easily resolved by the Security Council because all mandates are ultimately based on its authority.

Every mandate should be sufficiently clear that the Force Commander understands what he is expected to accomplish. But a more fundamental issue is *feasibility:* Can the peace force reasonably be expected to accomplish the tasks contained in the mandate? Some tasks may yield to a more capable peace force than was originally planned. Others may be inherently so difficult that even a very capable peace force will be frustrated.

Mandates also imply rules of engagement. Critics of peace operations often claim that the rules of engagement are too restrictive. In fact, the rules have usually allowed harder measures than Force Commanders dared to take, in view of their forces' vulnerability. Finally, the Security Council needs to consider conditions for terminating an operation. If the Council decides to terminate when the mandate is accomplished, it can be trapped into an interminable operation, waiting for the parties to fulfill their parts. To avoid this trap, the Council may simply set a deadline, putting the parties on notice that they have only a limited time to make use of the opportunities afforded by the peace operation.

## Character of the Peace Force

Is the peace force configured appropriately for its mandate? As with any military force, a peace force should be properly armed, equipped, and controlled to accomplish its mission, or, in the context of peace operations, its mandate. Appropriate configuration can vary from unarmed observers to a heavily armed combined task force.

Issues concerning the peace force include capabilities, size, composition, and control. The Secretary-General often has difficulty assembling a force with the required capabilities, especially transport, engineers, and medical units, unless great powers are enthusiastic participants. The force should be sized appropriately for its tasks and area of operations. Its composition by national contingent should ensure impartiality and efficiency. In recent years, the Council has departed significantly from its traditional practice of excluding contributors notoriously sympathetic to one side. Had it not departed from this principle, France would have been excluded from Rwanda, and the United States and Russia would have been excluded from Bosnia-Herzegovina. In these examples, impartiality was maintained, but the new practice harbors a risk that peace forces might join in the conflict.

Control over combat operations is a central issue for any peace force operating under Chapter VII. The U.N. system is not suitable to control combat operations, because member states have not fully implemented relevant articles of the Charter and are unlikely to do so. Therefore, when the Security Council invokes Chapter VII, it should select some agent, usually a lead state or regional alliance, that can control combat operations effectively. The Security Council often authorizes U.N.–controlled operations simultaneously or sequentially with operations controlled by its agents. In such cases, the operations should be properly related to each other.

## Physical Environment

How will physical environment affect the operation? Peace operations have taken place in some of the world's most inhospitable, rugged, and densely forested terrain, greatly impeding operations. The physical environment affects peace operations across the spectrum, but the specific effects vary according to the type of operation.

What effects will climate and terrain have on the operation? How will the availability of infrastructure, such as airports, seaports, and road networks, affect it?  What facilities will the parties make available? What facilities must be constructed, improved, or repaired?

## Extent of International Support

Will states that are not parties adequately support the operation? *Support* includes voting affirmatively, participating in the operation, and applying political pressure on the parties to keep their agreements.

Some states, exemplified by Canada and the Scandinavian countries, participate in traditional peace-keeping because they are morally and ideologically committed to the principles of the Charter.  In addition, some states view peace-keeping as a way to increase their prestige and improve relations with great powers.

But motives that suffice for peace-keeping may not be adequate for Chapter VII operations, including peace enforcement, with its inherent risk of casualties.  To participate in such operations, states may have to believe that their geopolitical interests justify such a high level of involvement.  For example, U.S. willingness to lead the Implementation Force (IFOR) is heavily conditioned by the U.S. role in NATO and U.S. concern with the stability of Eastern Europe. There is an underlying tension in peace operations at the high end: Participating states must have enough interest to justify the monetary cost and risk to their troops, yet be sufficiently disinterested to maintain impartiality.

Critical issues include support from the five permanent members of the Security Council, the United States as a national actor, and regional powers that have political influence on the parties.  In all cases, the Permanent Five must be willing to approve the mandate, but at the high end of peace operations they also have to generate a robust consensus for action.  Discord among the Permanent Five can cause protracted frustration, as demonstrated in the Congo and, more recently, in Bosnia-Herzegovina.  U.S. participation, discussed broadly in Chapter Two, is always critical for peace enforcement and sometimes also for less-demanding operations.  Finally, regional powers often exert strong influence on peace operations by supporting sanctions, especially arms embargoes, and by keeping political pressure on the parties to stay within the peace process.

## REFORMING PEACE OPERATIONS

Since the end of the Cold War, the Security Council has authorized more-extensive and more-ambitious peace operations, including several efforts at peace enforcement. While conducting these operations, the Council has suffered spectacular and humiliating failures that have overshadowed successes in lesser peace operations and have eroded the prestige of the Security Council.

To prevent the recurrence of such failures and recover prestige, the Council should resolve the issues presented in this report. The Security Council should carefully judge the stage of conflict and not try to conduct peace operations when the parties do not want peace. It should hold parties to their word and not obscure the central issue of consent by allowing them to maintain a pretense. It should ensure that mandates are feasible, especially considering the peace force. Most important, it should make operations consonant with the political will of its own members. The United States cannot effect these reforms alone. However, as the leading state, it bears the greatest share of responsibility.

### Judging the Stage of Conflict

Peace operations, even those conducted under Chapter VII, presuppose that the conflict has reached a stage that the parties believe is conclusive. If, to the contrary, parties believe that they can still advance their interests by fighting, then even a successful Chapter VII operation can gain only momentary respite.

Too frequently, the Security Council has launched or continued peace operations despite strong indications that the parties intended to go on fighting. In Lebanon, the hapless peace force is largely irrelevant to a protracted conflict between Hezbollah and Israeli forces. Somalia is still not ripe for any peace operation short of forcible disarmament of the warring clans. The factions in Liberia are fighting primarily for loot and seem to regard the international community as an additional victim to plunder. The conflict in the former Yugoslavia was little amenable to peace operations until the Croats had attained most of their war aims and the Bosnian Serbs had suffered reverses—in other words, until the conflict had reached a culminating point.

Admittedly, there are strong pressures on the Security Council to continue even those operations that have long been failing. Member states initiate peace operations because they feel that something should be done. To terminate operations while the conflict is still raging implies that nothing can be done, that the Council has decided to leave not just the parties, but peoples, to their fate. Very often, terminating peace operations will also diminish the ability of non-governmental agencies to deliver humanitarian aid. Given these conflicting motives, it is not surprising that each new agreement among the parties nourishes hope that a turning point may yet be reached. But if the Security Council is to regain prestige, it must be quicker to recognize when conflicts are not amenable to peace operations and decline to authorize them. The United States should help to instill this more realistic outlook.

## Holding Parties to Their Word

The issue of consent, so central to all peace operations, should not be obscured by allowing parties to offer a pretense of consent while they actually subvert the mandate. Of course, actual consent is likely to fall short of the formal consent manifested in agreements. It would be unrealistic to expect that parties, especially those involved in civil conflict, would maintain the precise letter of their agreements. On the contrary, most parties will usually try to twist agreements in ways favorable to themselves and commit violations. But at some point, the Security Council must hold the parties to their word or risk humiliation.

It is especially important that the Council draw a clear line between consent and recalcitrance. At a minimum, attacking the peace force or holding its personnel hostage should be regarded as evidence that a party does not support the mandate, with important consequences for the peace operation. So long as the parties maintain their consent to the operation, the peace force should expect to be treated as a nonbelligerent, as symbolized by blue helmets. When any party becomes recalcitrant, blue helmets serve no useful purpose; indeed, they are worse than useless.

The worst failures, especially in Bosnia-Herzegovina, Croatia, Liberia, and Somalia, have occurred because the Council accepted a pretense of consent from parties who did not actually support the mandate. In several instances, most lamentably in Bosnia-Herzegovina, the Council allowed peace forces to operate in a confusing twilight zone, ostensibly with consent and actually at the mercy of recalcitrant parties. Whether or not its own troops participate, the United States should insist that parties be held to their word.

## Ensuring That Mandates Are Feasible

When framing mandates, the Security Council should carefully evaluate the feasibility of those mandates, especially considering the limited forces that member states are usually willing to contribute. Too often, the Council has issued mandates that overtaxed the peace force, even though permanent members of the Council participated. To be taken seriously by belligerent parties, the Council must ensure that its words do not outrun its deeds. For example, during the Rwanda crisis in April 1994, the United States helped ensure that the Council avoided mandates that were not feasible, despite political pressures to take a more active role.

The Security Council lacks immediate access to a military staff that could plan large-scale (multi-battalion) peace operations and estimate the required forces. Indeed, it is doubtful whether such a staff should be created within the United Nations system, even assuming that there were support for the proposal. Therefore, whenever large-scale operations are contemplated, the Council should turn to an outside agent, as, for example, NATO in the case of IFOR. Considering its historical role in peace operations and its unrivaled military power, the United States is most likely to take the lead in this planning, unilaterally, within NATO, or as leader of an ad hoc coalition.

## Making Operations Consonant with Political Will

Most important, the Security Council should make peace operations consonant with the political will of member states, especially that of its own permanent members. It seems strange that permanent members would pass resolutions exceeding their political will; yet, undeniably, they have done so, most notoriously in the former Yugoslavia. There is an enormous gap between the potential power of the Council, essentially perpetuating the victorious alliance of World War II, and its actual power, which may be negligible. To realize its potential power, the Council must generate a consensus for action, which is analogous to an alliance, that reflects the political will of its members. Absent such consensus, the Council becomes powerless and its resolutions—mere exhortations that the parties can defy without ill consequences to themselves—command no more respect than those of the General Assembly.

Within the Security Council, the United States is primus inter pares, its policy often essential to building consensus. Its leading role is especially apparent in Chapter VII operations, whether or not they ultimately entail peace enforcement. No other state could have led Chapter VII peace operations in Africa (Somalia), the Western Hemisphere (Haiti), and Europe (Bosnia-Herzegovina). When the United States supports an operation, especially through its own participation, other member states are drawn into the endeavor. When the United States displays disinterest or irresolution, no other state can repair the lack.

It is unrealistic to expect that some nebulous entity such as the international community will be able to conduct Chapter VII operations successfully. For such operations, the United States should expect to lead other willing states as it has done in cases of enforcement against aggressors. If the United States itself lacks political will or cannot elicit enough support, it should prevent the Council from invoking Chapter VII rather than approve peace operations that are likely to fail and further discredit the Council.

# ACKNOWLEDGMENTS

The authors gratefully acknowledge the help of colleagues at RAND. Arnold Kanter and Greg Treverton provided overall guidance. As leader of "Operational Strategies for Peace Enforcement," Bruce Bennett helped to provide the intellectual framework. Within that project, Arthur Bullock prepared very helpful case studies of peace operations in Cambodia and the Congo. Ted Karasik conducted research into peace operations, especially decisions of the Security Council. Richard Darilek contributed insights into peace operations on the Golan Heights. Stephen Hosmer commented on peace operations from his wide understanding of military affairs. Dean Millot advised on points of international law. Marten van Heuven reviewed the initial draft of this document.

The head of RAND's Washington office, David Chu, helped to finance Bruce Pirnie's participation in a tour of peace operations in the former Yugoslavia during June 3–10, 1994, which was conducted by the United Nations Association of the United States. Nothing in this report should be construed as criticism of those who served under the U.N. flag in the former Yugoslavia. Their bravery and perseverance in very difficult circumstances deserve our respect.

The authors extend thanks to Sarah B. Sewall, Deputy Assistant Secretary of Defense for Peacekeeping and Peace Enforcement Policy, for her constructive criticism throughout the project, and for sponsoring a series of briefings that provoked helpful comments. Those briefings were given to interested persons in the U.N. Department of Peace-Keeping Operations, U.S. State Department, U.S. Mission to the United Nations, National Security Council,

Central Intelligence Agency, Department of Defense, Joint Staff, Defense Intelligence Agency, Army Staff, and the U.S. Army Training and Doctrine Command at Fort Monroe, Virginia.

They thank Lee Feinstein, the very model of an enthusiastic and capable project monitor; Leonard Hawley and Kenneth Handelman for offering constructive criticism and assisting in the series of briefings; Arthur Bullock for reviewing the final draft of this report; and their editor, Marian Branch, for her expert work, which greatly improved the report. Errors are the authors' responsibility.

# ACRONYMS AND ABBREVIATIONS

| | |
|---|---|
| AMC | Air Mobility Command |
| ARFOR | Army Force [service component] |
| AWACS | Airborne Warning and Control System |
| CINCUNC | Commander in Chief, United Nations Command [Korea] |
| CJCS | Chairman, Joint Chiefs of Staff |
| CMO | Chief Military Observer |
| CMOC | Civil-Military Operations Center |
| CRS | Congressional Research Service |
| DPKO | Department of Peace-Keeping Operations |
| ECOMOG | ECOWAS Monitoring Group [in Liberia] |
| ECOWAS | Economic Community of West African States [established by treaty to promote economic integration and political cooperation among 15 West African nations] |
| FMLN | *Frente Farabundo Martí para la Liberación Nacional* |
| FSS | Fast sealift ship |
| FUNCINPEC | United Front for an Independent, Neutral, Peaceful, and Cooperative Cambodia [Royalist party] |
| GAO | General Accounting Office |
| HOC | Humanitarian Operations Center |

| | |
|---|---|
| IFOR | Implementation Force [in the former Yugoslavia to implement the Dayton Agreements] |
| JCS | Joint Chiefs of Staff |
| KPNLF | Khmer People's National Liberation Front [alliance of pro–Lon Nol elements] |
| LASH | Lighter aboard ship [a flat-bottomed boat for use near shore; also referred to as *lighterage*] |
| MINURSO | United Nations Mission for the Referendum in Western Sahara [September 1991–present] |
| MNF | Multinational Force [Haiti] |
| NATO | North Atlantic Treaty Organization |
| NGO | Non-governmental organization |
| OAS | Organization of American States |
| OAU | Organization of African Unity |
| ONUC | *Operation des Nations Unies au Congo* [former Belgian Congo, July 1960–June 1964] |
| ONUCA | United Nations Observer Group in Central America [Costa Rica, El Salvador, Guatemala, Honduras, Nicaragua; November 1989–January 1992] |
| ONUMOZ | United Nations Operation in Mozambique [December 1992–December 1994] |
| ONUSAL | United Nations Observer Mission in El Salvador [July 1991–present] |
| PDK | Party of Democratic Kampuchea [Pol Pot faction of Khmer Rouge] |
| PLO | Palestine Liberation Organization |
| [*Frente*] POLISARIO | *Frente Popular para la Liberación de Saguia el-Hamra y de Rio de Oro* [an independence movement that declared the Sahrawi Arab Democratic Republic in the Western Sahara] |
| RPF | Rwandan Patriotic Front [Tutsi-dominated political-military organization] |
| RPG | Rocket-propelled grenade |

| | |
|---|---|
| SACEUR | Supreme Allied Commander in Europe |
| SC | Security Council |
| SRSG | Special Representative of the Secretary-General |
| SWAPO | South West African People's Organization |
| U.N. | United Nations |
| UNAMIC | United Nations Advance Mission in Cambodia |
| UNAMIR | United Nations Assistance Mission in Rwanda [October 1993–present] |
| UNAVEM I | First United Nations Angola Verification Mission [January 1989–June 1991] |
| UNAVEM II | Second United Nations Angola Verification Mission [June 1991–February 1995] |
| UNAVEM III | Third United Nations Angola Verification Mission [February 1995–present] |
| UNCRO | United Nations Confidence Restoration Operation in Croatia |
| UNDOF | United Nations Disengagement Observer Force [Golan Heights, June 1974–present] |
| UNEF I | First United Nations Emergency Force [Gaza and Sinai, November 1956–June 1967] |
| UNEF II | Second United Nations Emergency Force [Sinai, October 1973–July 1979] |
| UNFICYP | United Nations Peace-Keeping Force in Cyprus [March 1964–present] |
| UNGOMAP | United Nations Good Offices Mission in Afghanistan and Pakistan [April 1988–March 1990] |
| UNHCR | United Nations High Commissioner for Refugees |
| UNICEF | United Nations Children's Fund |
| UNIFIL | United Nations Interim Force in Lebanon [March 1978–present] |
| UNIIMOG | United Nations Iran-Iraq Military Observer Group [August 1988–February 1991] |

| UNIKOM | United Nations Iraq-Kuwait Observer Mission [April 1991–present] |
| UNITA | *União Nacional para a Independência Total de Angola* [National Union for the Complete Independence of Angola] |
| UNITAF | Unified Task Force [Somalia] |
| UNMIBH | United Nations Mission in Bosnia and Herzegovina [February 1996–present] |
| UNMIH | United Nations Mission in Haiti [September 1993–present] |
| UNMOGIP | United Nations Military Observer Group in India and Pakistan [Jammu and Kashmir, January 1949–present] |
| UNOGIL | United Nations Observation Group in Lebanon [June 1958–December 1958] |
| UNOMIL | United Nations Observer Mission in Liberia [September 1993–present] |
| UNOMUR | United Nations Observer Mission Uganda-Rwanda [June 1993–September 1994] |
| UNOSOM I | First United Nations Operation in Somalia [April 1992–April 1993] |
| UNOSOM II | Second United Nations Operation in Somalia [May 1993–March 1995] |
| UNPREDEP | United Nations Preventive Deployment Force [Macedonia] |
| UNPROFOR | United Nations Protection Force [the former Yugoslavia, March 1992–December 1995] |
| UNSC | United Nations Security Council |
| UNSF | United Nations Security Force in West New Guinea (West Irian) [October 1962–April 1963] |
| UNTAC | United Nations Transitional Authority in Cambodia [March 1992–September 1993] |
| UNTAG | United Nations Transition Assistance Group [Namibia, April 1989–March 1990] |

| | |
|---|---|
| UNTSO | United Nations Truce Supervision Organization [Near East, June 1948–present] |
| UNYOM | United Nations Yemen Observation Mission [Saudi-Yemen border, July 1963–September 1964] |
| U.S. | United States |
| USCENTCOM | United States Central Command |
| USCINCCENT | United States Commander in Chief, Central Command |
| USFORSOM | United States Forces in Somalia |
| WFP | World Food Program |
| WHO | World Health Organization |
| WWII | World War II |

# Chapter One

# INTRODUCTION

As a power with global interests, the United States has a strong concern for successful peace operations. Seldom if ever will its interests be well served by failures, especially widely publicized and expensive failures that tend to discredit the United Nations. This report develops issues associated with peace operations conducted under authority of the United Nations, either through the United Nations system or by other agents. At the outset, it offers commentary on questions raised by *The Clinton Administration's Policy on Reforming Multilateral Peace Operations*[1] (hereafter *Administration's Policy*): Should the United States vote affirmatively? Should the United States participate with its own personnel? Every member state with a seat on the Security Council must answer the first question, and many member states will also have to consider whether they should contribute troops. But U.S. decisions carry the greatest weight and are often critical, especially its decision to participate. When the United States decides to participate in a peace operation, its immense power and prestige radically increase the chances for success.

To correctly answer the questions raised by *Administration's Policy*, U.S. decisionmakers should resolve issues that are associated with every peace operation: the character of the conflict, consent of the parties, mandate, peace force, physical environment, and extent of international support. In certain cases, some of these issues cannot be resolved unless the United States participates. For example, it is

---

[1]U.S. Department of State, *The Clinton Administration's Policy on Reforming Multilateral Peace Operations*, Washington, D.C., Publication 10161, May 1994.

highly doubtful whether the military provisions of the Dayton Agreements could have been enforced successfully unless U.S. ground forces were deployed in Bosnia-Herzegovina. In all cases, U.S. decisionmakers should resolve these issues before deciding how to vote in the Security Council, thereby ensuring that peace operations have a reasonable prospect of success.

## WHAT ARE PEACE OPERATIONS?

Peace operations are defined[2] by consent of the parties and impartiality of the Security Council. In authorizing peace operations, the Security Council has invoked Chapter VI and Chapter VII of the United Nations Charter.[3] The spectrum of peace operation extends from observation at the low (in cost and risk) end to peace enforcement at the high end.

### Consent and Impartiality

Peace operations are not derived from doctrine or theory; rather, they are derived ad hoc, from the exigencies of conflict situations.[4] Reflecting this origin, peace operations have often been vaguely or confusingly defined, even by U.N. officials. They have two essential characteristics: consent of the parties and impartiality on the part of the Security Council.

*Consent* is the manifest willingness of parties to cooperate in accomplishing the mandate. Parties may subsequently withdraw their consent; however, to date, no peace operation has begun without initial consent. If, for example, the United States had invaded Haiti by force in late 1994, that operation would have been *enforcement* under authority of the Security Council, not a peace operation.[5]

---

[2]See Appendix A for definitions of terms used in this study.

[3]United Nations, *Charter of the United Nations*, San Francisco, Calif., June 25, 1945.

[4]United Nations, *The Blue Helmets: A Review of United Nations Peace-Keeping*, Department of Public Information, New York, 1990, p. 4.

[5]As events actually occurred, the Cédras regime consented reluctantly at the eleventh hour, under threat of invasion by overwhelmingly superior U.S. forces. Haiti offers an extreme example of consent under duress, but consent is usually conditioned by expectations that force might be used—if not by great powers, then by other parties to

*Impartiality* implies that the Security Council does not take sides, because it judges that all parties share responsibility for a conflict.[6] However, it does not imply that every action taken by the Security Council during a peace operation will affect all parties equally. Indeed, even the least intrusive peace operation is unlikely to affect all parties equally.

## Chapter VI and Chapter VII

Peace operations are not described in the Charter.[7] They would seem to fall somewhere between Chapter VI (Pacific Settlement of Disputes) and Chapter VII (Action with Respect to Threats to the Peace, Breaches of the Peace, and Acts of Aggression). The Security Council usually invokes Chapter VI, implying that lethal force will be used only in self-defense while accomplishing the mandate.[8] When the Security Council invokes Chapter VII, it implies that lethal force may be used beyond self-defense, potentially to coerce a party.[9]

---

the conflict. The Aristide government quite naturally consented to a peace operation that was intended to restore and uphold its authority. After restoration of the Aristide government, impartiality became irrelevant, because there were no more parties, only the sole legitimate government.

[6]If, on the other hand, the Security Council holds that one party bears sole responsibility for the conflict, it might authorize sanctions and enforcement without qualification, rather than "peace enforcement." In this case, the Security Council has no obligation to be impartial. On the contrary, it directs enforcement against the aggressor that bears sole responsibility; e.g., Iraq was solely responsible for invading Kuwait in 1990.

[7]However, Secretary-General Boutros Boutros-Ghali has attempted to construct a typology. See Appendix B for analysis of the Secretary-General's reports to the Security Council on this subject, known under the short title *Agenda for Peace*.

[8]The traditional rule of engagement for peace-keepers is self-defense while accomplishing the mandate, implying more than just self-protection. If, for example, an interposition force were deployed on key terrain, self-defense might mean denying that terrain to all parties. Exactly this case occurred when the United Nations Peace-Keeping Force in Cyprus (UNFICYP) occupied Nicosia Airport in July 1974 and confronted advancing Turkish forces.

[9]The Security Council has given the same broad authorization to employ force under Chapter VII in impartial peace enforcement as in enforcement against a unique aggressor. For example, Security Council Resolution 678 on November 29, 1990, authorized action against Iraq as follows: "Acting under Chapter VII of the Charter of the United Nations, . . . 2. Authorizes Member States . . . to use all necessary means to uphold and implement Security Council Resolution 660 [demanding withdrawal of Iraqi forces from Kuwait]." Similarly, Security Council Resolution 940 on July 31, 1994, authorized action against the Cédras regime in Haiti as follows: "Acting under Chapter

## Spectrum of Peace Operations[10]

From an operational perspective, the Security Council has authorized five types of peace operations:  observation, interposition, transition, security for humanitarian aid, and peace enforcement.  Figure 1.1 displays these types in a spectrum of peace operations.

**Peace-Keeping.**  Peace-keeping includes observation and interposition conducted under Chapter VI.  *Observation* involves monitoring

RAND*MR583-1.1*

| Peace Operations | | | | | | | |
|---|---|---|---|---|---|---|---|
| Peace-Keeping | | | | More-Ambitious Operations | | | |
| Observation | | Interposition | | Transition | | Security for Humanitarian Aid | Peace Enforcement |
| Facilitate agreement | Deter violations | Facilitate agreement | Deter violations | | | | |
| **Chapter of the U.N. Charter** | Chapter VI (self-defense) | | | Chapter VI (self-defense) | Chapter VII (potential enforcement) | Chapter VII (secure aid) | Chapter VII (enforce will of UNSC) |
| **Consent Required from the Parties** | Allow access to observers | | Acquiesce in impartial control of a buffer zone | | Cooperate in achieving new condition and status of a country | | Allow provision of aid | None: occurs when party *withdraws* consent |
| **Typical Mandate** | Observe compliance with agreements; report violations; mediate among parties | Plus respond forcefully to violations | Create buffer zones; control entry into buffer zones; monitor arms limitations | Plus respond forcefully to violations | Provide secure conditions; oversee demobilization, demilitarization, arms limitations; provide security for electoral activities; facilitate reconstruction; cooperate closely with civilian component and NGOs | | Provide security for humanitarian aid | Coerce recalcitrant parties into complying with UNSC resolutions and parties' agreements |

|←————————— Chapter VI —————————→|←————— Chapter VII —————→|

Figure 1.1—Spectrum of Peace Operations

---

VII of the Charter of the United Nations, authorizes Member States to form a multinational force under unified command and control and, in this framework, *to use all necessary means* to facilitate the departure from Haiti of the military leadership, consistent with the Governors Island Agreement" [emphasis added].

[10]See Bruce R. Pirnie and William E. Simons, *Soldiers for Peace:  An Operational Typology,* RAND, Santa Monica, Calif., MR-582-OSD, 1996, for an exposition and discussion of the spectrum of peace operations.

compliance with agreements, reporting violations, and mediating resolution of violations. *Interposition* requires the peace force to control a buffer zone between the opposing parties. Peace-keeping has usually been intended to facilitate agreements, leaving the onus for keeping the agreements on the parties. But in two cases (Macedonia, Kuwait), peace-keeping was intended to deter violations ("preventive deployment"),[11] which implies that the Security Council would respond forcefully if violations occurred.

**More-Ambitious Operations.** More-ambitious operations, especially prevalent since the end of the Cold War, include transition, security for humanitarian aid, and peace enforcement. *Transition operations* are intended to change the condition and status of a country by, for example, reconciling warring parties within a new governmental structure. More narrowly, the Council may decide to *secure humanitarian aid*, thus alleviating suffering caused by conflict. *Peace enforcement* has ensued when parties withdrew consent during operations conducted under Chapter VII and the Security Council attempted to coerce them.

## Intervention in Internal Crises

According to its Charter, the first purpose of the United Nations is "to maintain international peace and security" (Article 1). It is enjoined not to intervene "in matters which are essentially within the domestic jurisdiction of any state" (Article 2). But the distinction between *international relations* and *domestic jurisdiction* is not always clear, as the former Yugoslavia illustrates: The Security Council and a Contact Group of great powers promoted a plan to effectively partition Bosnia-Herzegovina, a member state in the United Nations, among Croats, Muslims, and Serbs.[12] Thus, the parties to a conflict

---

[11]"Preventive deployment" reflects current usage in the United Nations, e.g., the United Nations *Preventive Deployment* Force in Macedonia; however, this term is a misnomer. *Prevent* means to stop someone from doing something or to stop something from happening, but a peace-keeping force does not have such power; it cannot prevent violations, but only provide timely, reliable notice that violations have occurred.

[12]Croats and Muslims will share roughly half of Bosnia-Herzegovina under the current agreement, but few observers expect these nationalities to cooperate in establishing a multinational federation.

within a recognized state were treated as peoples with rights to self-determination, as guaranteed in Article 1 of the Charter.

As a practical matter, the Security Council has expanded the definition of *international peace and security* to include such phenomena as refugee flows and catastrophic suffering. In Somalia, for example, the Security Council responded to catastrophic suffering by assuming a broad authority to promote establishment of a new national government. In Haiti, the Security Council undertook to restore the legitimate government, in part because refugee flows burdened neighboring states.

## ROLE OF THE UNITED STATES

The United States is involved in every peace operation conducted under authority of the U.N., even when it decides not to participate with combat forces. As a permanent member of the Security Council, the United States has veto power; therefore, every peace operation must have at least its tacit approval. As the wealthiest member state, it is required to pay the largest assessment for peace operations. In addition, the United States is frequently asked to provide unique or superior capabilities, such as global airlift and sealift.

As a world power with global responsibilities, the United States is also concerned with its prestige. It may participate in peace-keeping without risking prestige, because the onus for maintaining agreements is on the parties. But when the United States decides to participate in more-ambitious operations, its prestige will be affected by the outcome. If it appears irresolute or easily discouraged in an ambitious peace operation, especially peace enforcement, it will lose prestige, which will diminish the United States' ability to advance its own interests elsewhere in the world.

## CHECKLIST OF CRITICAL ISSUES

This report is intended to assist the analysis of peace operations. It provides a checklist of critical issues that should be resolved when a new peace operation is proposed or an existing operation is under review. We offer *issues* rather than *guidelines*, because peace operations are too complex and too highly variable to follow a tidy set of guidelines. The rich experience of peace operations, including that of some current operations whose outcome remains uncertain, demonstrates what issues are critical.

The checklist is organized around six headings that cover the subject of peace operations:

- Amenability of the conflict to peace operations
- Consent of parties bearing responsibility for the conflict
- The mandate approved by the Security Council
- Configuration of the peace force
- Physical environment surrounding the operation
- Extent of international support for the operation.

Under each heading, we pose one broad issue, essentially a starting point for inquiry. Then we divide each broad issue into several subsumed issues that form the checklist. The checklist is designed to be applicable universally, but each critical issue assumes different dimensions according to the type of operation that is being contemplated or is in progress.

How amenable is this conflict to peace operations in general and, more specifically, to the type of operation that is contemplated? (See Chapter Three.) Distinguishing the degree of amenability demands expert judgment, usually in a complex political-military situation. Within the bounds of this brief study, we merely outline the subsumed issues: the stage that the conflict has reached, prevalence of unconventional warfare, presence of irreconcilable aims or virulent animosity, the degree of central control that parties exert over their forces, and inherent risk to personnel in the peace force. For example, the parties in Liberia have so little control that some militia, including drugged and intoxicated children, are really just marauders. To the extent that the parties have lost control of their supporters, their consent to peace plans is meaningless, even if given in good faith.

How much consent can be expected from the parties? (See Chapter Four.) In other words, how willing are the parties to help accomplish the mandate? Consent provides an initial foundation for all peace operations, even those that eventually become peace enforcement. At the outset, it is important to understand how much consent will be required from the parties to ensure a successful operation. They might be expected merely to cease fire while retaining their military power, or to disarm and demobilize their forces, thus surrendering power. In Liberia, for example, the parties have repeatedly agreed to disarm and demobilize under supervision of the peace force, implying a very high degree of consent if they were negotiating in good faith. Does consent currently appear adequate, bearing in mind that formal consent and actual consent may be very different? What are the prospects for maintaining consent throughout the peace process? And finally, what options should be prepared for in the event that one or more parties were to withdraw consent, even to the extent of attacking the peace force?

Does the mandate well define the purpose and scope of the operation? (See Chapter Five.) Are the provisions of the mandate clearly expressed? In political affairs, vagueness may often be salutary, but a mandate must translate into the mission of the peace force. A vague mandate would place the Special Representative of the Secretary-General and the Force Commander in the untenable position of guessing at the intentions of the Council. But clarity is no guarantee of success. A more fundamental issue is feasibility, considering the anticipated peace force: Can the peace force reasonably be expected to accomplish the provisions of the mandate? In Liberia, for example, the peace force as currently constituted may not be able to forcefully disarm militias, even within a limited geographic area. Are the rules of engagement appropriate to the circumstances and to the intent of the Council? Finally, does the mandate set forth conditions to terminate the operation and, if not, is an open-ended, potentially interminable operation acceptable?

Is the peace force configured appropriately for its mandate? (See Chapter Six.) As in any military operation, the peace force should have the required capabilities and size. Required capabilities vary widely, according to the type of operation. The appropriate size is affected by the area of operations, the tasks implied by the mandate, and, in Chapter VII operations, by the level and extent of opposition that might be encountered. Since peace operations are normally conducted by multinational forces, composition by national contingents can be an important issue. For example, in Liberia the peace force is dominated by the Nigerian contingent, whose impartiality is at least questionable. Finally, there is the difficult issue of controlling the peace force. At the low end of peace operations, control may be immediate and personal, generating little requirement for complex organization or experienced staff. But at the high end, especially during peace enforcement, sophisticated and highly responsive control mechanisms may be essential for success.

How is the physical environment likely to influence operations? (See Chapter Seven.) Climate, terrain, and available infrastructure all affect the chances for success, often in very adverse ways. Peace operations have been conducted in some of the world's most inhospitable terrain, from the vast jungles of the Congo to the jagged mountains of Afghanistan. Very often, infrastructure, including seaports, airports, and internal transportation, has been poorly developed or entirely absent. Such harsh environments can make even observation extremely difficult and impede the operations of the most modern military forces.

Will member states that are not parties to the conflict adequately support the peace operation? (See Chapter Eight.) Every peace operation requires support within the Security Council, including, of course, that of the five permanent members who have veto power. For peace operations at the low end, it may suffice for the five permanent members to share a general willingness to address the conflict, whereas, at the high end, they must agree more precisely on a course of action. The most important issue may be participation by the United States, which is often linked to U.S. interests that may be variously defined or highly contentious. In addition, support from regional powers may be crucial. In the case of Liberia, for example, some regional states have permitted or even encouraged arms shipments to the parties in contravention of the arms embargo.

# Chapter Two

# COMMENTARY ON *ADMINISTRATION'S POLICY*

The standards in *Administration's Policy* should be interpreted with subtlety, not applied mechanically as ascending thresholds.[1]

## APPLYING *ADMINISTRATION'S POLICY*

*Administration's Policy* sets standards for (1) an affimative vote in the Security Council, (2) U.S. participation, and (3) U.S. participation in operations under Chapter VII. The same criteria appear in several standards, but they change meanings in each context. For example, advancing U.S. interest is a criterion in all three standards, but U.S. interests that would justify an affirmative vote (standard 1) might not justify U.S. participation (standard 2), and those that justify U.S. participation might not be strong enough to justify participation in a Chapter VII operation (standard 3). Therefore, this criterion should be interpreted differently in the context of each standard. Other criteria, including clarity of objectives, domestic support, and control arrangements, should also be interpreted differently in the context of different standards.

Relationships among operations may also affect the evaluation. For example, if the United States contemplates a unilateral operation with hand-off to a multilateral operation, it should consider these operations in relationship to each other, not in isolation.

---

[1]See Appendix C for a summary of the standards and the associated criteria contained in *Administration's Policy* (U.S. Department of State, 1994).

It is doubtful that the standard for an affirmative vote is adequate for a combat operation without U.S. participation, as a literal reading of *Administration's Policy* would suggest.  On the contrary, it would seem advisable to apply the most rigorous standard whenever combat operations are contemplated; otherwise, the risk of failure will be high, as it was for U.N. troops in Somalia after the United States unilaterally withdrew its forces.  Failure in any operation, whether or not the United States participated, will usually injure U.S. interests, at least its declared interest in the United Nations as an effective instrument for collective action.

Moreover, it appears that criteria for U.S. participation in Chapter VII operations should be applied to lesser operations.  For example, the criterion "commit sufficient forces to achieve clearly defined objectives" should apply to any peace operation.

## SHOULD THE UNITED STATES VOTE AFFIRMATIVELY?

*Administration's Policy* sets forth eight criteria for deciding whether to vote for a proposed peace operation.

### U.S. Interests and Community of Interest

"UN involvement advances U.S. interests, and there is an international community of interest for dealing with the problem on a multilateral basis."[2]

**U.S. Interests.**  The United States has broadly defined national goals, such as promoting respect for human rights, that coincide with its obligations as a founding member of the U.N.[3]  These broadly defined goals might be adduced to justify almost any imaginable peace operation.  But neither the United States nor the U.N. can afford to approve operations indiscriminately.

---

[2]This and subsequent quotations delineating the eight criteria are from *Administration's Policy.*

[3]"To reaffirm faith in fundamental human rights, in the dignity and worth of the human person, in the equal rights of men and women and of nations large and small...." Preamble to the *Charter of the United Nations.*

The United States also has more closely defined objectives, which are expressed in its national security strategy and its national military strategy.  Its willingness to approve an operation, especially more-ambitious peace operations and every case of peace enforcement, should be linked to these objectives.  Absent this linkage, domestic support will probably be fragile, as evidenced by Somalia.

The United States has often advanced specific geopolitical interests[4] through peace operations.  For example, UNFICYP helped to avert war between Greece and Turkey, two NATO allies whose rivalry threatened to disrupt NATO's southern flank during the Cold War.  As another example, the United Nations Good Offices Mission in Afghanistan and Pakistan (UNGOMAP) confirmed the departure of Soviet troops from Afghanistan, a long-standing goal of U.S. policy.

**Community of Interest.**  A community of interest will sustain less-expensive and less-risky peace-keeping, but some more-ambitious peace operations and all peace enforcement require a more robust consensus for action.   Consensus for action implies that the Permanent Five and other involved states share an understanding of what outcome is desirable, how that outcome can be achieved, what effort is required, and what states will sustain that effort.  See Chapter Eight for issues relating to international support.

In 1991, for example, 15 states other than the parties signed the Paris Agreement concerning Cambodia.  In effect, they formed a consensus to monitor compliance with the agreement and to facilitate its implementation, but not to coerce any party.  Therefore, when the Khmer Rouge withdrew from the peace process, the Special Representative of the Secretary-General (SRSG), Yasushi Akashi, had little alternative but to continue working with cooperative parties while largely ignoring the Khmer Rouge.

In Somalia, the United States attained a consensus for action through its leadership and willingness to participate.  Because that consensus depended critically on U.S. leadership, it dissolved when the United States changed its policy.  And with regard to Bosnia-Herzegovina from 1992 through late 1995, the Permanent Five con-

---

[4] *Geopolitical interests* are interests derived from power relationships among states, considering their areas, resources, and locations on the earth's surface.

spicuously failed to attain a consensus for action and therefore failed to conduct an effective operation.

## Threat to Peace and Security

"There is a threat to or breach of international peace and security, often of a regional character, defined as one or a combination of the following:

- International aggression, or;

- Urgent humanitarian disaster coupled with violence;

- Sudden interruption of established democracy or gross violation of human rights coupled with violence, or threat of violence."

The U.N. does not have to wait until peace and security are breached before it takes action. On the contrary, the Charter provides that the U.N. may act when peace and security are only threatened. The first listed purpose of the organization is to maintain international peace and security and to that end "take effective collective measures for the prevention and removal of *threats* to the peace" (Article 1, emphasis added).

Whether a state is threatening the peace or is acting to deter a potential adversary is not always obvious. Nor is it easy to devise practical measures to prevent or remove threats to the peace. Most peace operations have been a response to a breach of the peace, not to a mere threat. But in two cases, the Security Council has acted to counter threats: the United Nations Iraq-Kuwait Observation Mission (UNIKOM)[5] and the United Nations Preventive Deployment Force (UNPREDEP) in Macedonia. By indicating that the Security Council will respond strongly, these operations are meant to deter states from violating international borders.

**International Aggression.** The Charter identifies breaches of the peace and acts of aggression as circumstances that might prompt

---

[5]This operation was authorized after the Persian Gulf War in an attempt to deter Iraq from repeating aggression against Kuwait. During October 1994, Iraq deployed forces in a threatening way, eliciting a military response from the United States and several Persian Gulf states.

action under Chapter VII. An act of aggression is distinguished from other breaches of the peace by the identification of an entity (the aggressor) that bears sole responsibility for the conflict. Member states have the inherent right of individual or collective self-defense (Article 51). When they exercise this right against an aggressor, they do not acquire responsibility for the conflict.[6] When the Security Council identifies a party with sole responsibility, it may authorize military action against that aggressor. Such action will be enforcement, not an impartial peace operation—for example, Korea in 1950 and Kuwait in 1990.

In practice, it can be difficult to identify the aggressor. Who was the aggressor in the Six Day War? Were the Arab states aggressors because they were obviously preparing an overwhelming offensive, or was Israel an aggressor because it attacked preemptively? In this instance, Secretary-General U Thant noted the Arab responsibility for requesting withdrawal of the First United Nations Emergency Force (UNEF I) and for assembling forces on the armistice line, and the General Assembly declined to adopt a Soviet-sponsored resolution condemning Israel. Was there an aggressor in Bosnia-Herzegovina? Officials in the Clinton Administration and U.S. congressional leadership repeatedly stated that the Serb side was an aggressor; yet the United States approved an impartial peace operation based on the premise that all parties shared responsibility.

**Humanitarian Disaster Coupled with Violence.** The Charter announces a determination "to promote social progress and better standards of life" (Preamble). The U.N. pursues humanitarian goals through the United Nations High Commissioner for Refugees (UNHCR), specialized agencies within the U.N. system, and cooperative relationships with many non-governmental organizations (NGOs).

UNHCR, with headquarters in Geneva, was founded in 1951 to cope with the refugees and displaced persons of World War II (WWII). It administers an annual budget of approximately $1.2 billion and serves as an intermediary coordinating the work of NGOs. For sev-

---

[6]For example, the Republic of Korea did not become responsible when it exercised the right of self-defense in 1950, nor did Kuwait when it defended itself against Iraq in 1990. In both cases, the aggressor remained solely responsible.

eral years, UNHCR was the primary coordinator of humanitarian aid to civilians suffering from the conflict in the former Yugoslavia. Specialized agencies that may assist during humanitarian disasters include the World Health Organization (WHO), the World Food Program (WFP), and the United Nations Children's Fund (UNICEF). Among the many NGOs are such famous organizations as CARE International, the Red Cross and Red Crescent Societies, Caritas Internationalis, and *Médecins sans Frontières* (Doctors Without Borders).

Often humanitarian disasters are not just coupled with violence but, rather, are caused *by* violence. Civil conflict among nationalities and ethnic groups is especially likely to cause humanitarian disasters. In Somalia, clashes among clan-based militias disrupted the economy so badly that large-scale starvation occurred. In Rwanda, Hutus tried to annihilate Tutsis, then fled when a Tutsi resistance movement seized power, leading to terrible suffering in Hutu refugee camps. In Liberia, tribal militias looted the country and almost completely destroyed its economy, causing widespread misery and flight to neighboring countries. Victims of the protracted conflict in the former Yugoslavia included Muslim populations of besieged cities and Serb refugees from Croat offensives.

In all these conflicts, international organizations and NGOs were harrassed, obstructed, and sometimes plundered by the factions, either for the factions' own benefit or to prevent aid from reaching their rivals. Moreover, some of the humanitarian aid supplied soldiers rather than civilians, including Hutu militias in Zaire and combatants on all sides in Bosnia-Herzegovina.[7]

**Gross Violation of Human Rights.** The Charter makes "promoting and encouraging respect for human rights and for fundamental freedoms" (Article 1) a purpose of the U.N. and gives the General

---

[7]"Bosnian Serbs, in part because they had the fewest sources of recognition from an international community that labeled them the aggressors, were particularly inclined to subject UNHCR and UNPROFOR convoys to endless inspections and restrictions on their freedom of movement. More than half of all humanitarian aid went to support the war effort by feeding and supplying soldiers. Control over the distribution of aid was a primary basis of local power. . . ." Susan L. Woodward, *Balkan Tragedy: Chaos and Dissolution After the Cold War*, The Brookings Institution, Washington, D.C., 1995, p. 319.

Assembly power to "initiate studies and make recommendations" (Article 13) for the purpose of realizing human rights and fundamental freedoms. On December 10, 1948, the General Assembly adopted the Universal Declaration of Human Rights.[8] On December 16, 1966, acting to further the principles contained in the Declaration, the General Assembly offered for signature the International Covenant on Civil and Political Rights. The Covenant is a treaty that obligates parties to respect and to ensure the enumerated rights of all individuals under their jurisdiction. These rights include the right to liberty and security of person, freedom of thought and expression, freedom of religion, freedom of assembly, right to participate in government, and equal protection of the law. The United States and three other permanent members of the Security Council (Britain, France, and Russia) are parties to the Covenant.

The United States has also ratified the Convention on the Prevention and Punishment of the Crime of Genocide.[9] The Convention defines *genocide* as "acts committed with intent to destroy, in whole or in part, a national, ethnic, racial or religious group" (Article II). The enumerated acts include killing, causing serious bodily harm, inflicting conditions of life calculated to destroy, preventing births within the group, and forcibly transferring children of the group to another group. The Convention makes punishable not only genocide but

---

[8]The Universal Declaration of Human Rights was drafted by the Commission on Human Rights, a body set up by the Economic and Social Council, with President Franklin D. Roosevelt's widow, Eleanor Roosevelt, as its presiding officer. It contains language reminiscent of the U.S. Declaration of Independence, the U.S. Bill of Rights, and the wartime Atlantic Charter. It was adopted with 48 favorable votes and eight abstentions: the three Soviet votes (Soviet Union, Belorussia, Ukraine), Poland, Czechoslovakia, Yugoslavia, Saudi Arabia, and South Africa. "It has become the foundation for establishing obligatory legal norms to govern international behavior with regard to rights of individuals." Peter R. Baehr and Leon Gordenker, *The United Nations in the 1990s*, St. Martin's Press, New York, 1992, p. 103. Although highly influential, the Universal Declaration is a proclamation of the General Assembly that does not have the binding force of the Charter.

[9]The Convention on the Prevention and Punishment of the Crime of Genocide was adopted by the General Assembly on December 9, 1948, and came into force on January 12, 1951. Under Article I, states that ratify the Convention bind themselves to prevent and punish genocide.

also conspiracy to commit genocide, incitement, attempts, and complicity.

The Security Council has often failed to secure rights guaranteed under the Universal Declaration of Human Rights, the International Covenant on Civil and Political Rights, and the Convention on the Prevention and Punishment of the Crime of Genocide. Rwanda provides the most recent and notorious example. During April–June 1994, a Hutu-dominated regime committed genocide[10] against Tutsi citizens without provoking a forceful response, even though a U.N. peace operation was under way in Rwanda at the time.[11]

**Sudden Interruption of Democracy.** Under the Charter, there is no requirement that member states be democratically governed. Currently, one of the Permanent Five is not. But the Universal Declaration of Human Rights includes a detailed commitment to democracy. Therefore, the United States has legal grounds to promote democracy through peace operations under auspices of the U.N., as it does currently in Haiti.

------------

[10]In accordance with Security Council Resolution 935, an Independent Commission of Experts examined evidence of violations of international law in Rwanda. The Commission found that an estimated 500,000 unarmed civilians were murdered in Rwanda from April 6 to July 15, 1994. It found "overwhelming evidence to prove that acts of genocide against the Tutsi group were perpetrated by Hutu elements in a concerted, planned, and methodical way." The Commission concluded that these "mass exterminations" constituted genocide under the meaning of Article II of the Convention. United Nations, *Letter Dated 1 October 1994 from the Secretary-General Addressed to the President of the Security Council,* S/1994/1125, New York, October 4, 1994.

[11]When the massacres began on April 6, 1994, the United Nations Observer Mission Uganda-Rwanda (UNOMUR) was deployed in Rwanda with a strength of about 2,500. On April 21, the Security Council voted to remove most of these personnel to prevent them from being endangered in a conflict between the Hutu-dominated government and the Rwandan Patriotic Front, invading from Uganda. On May 16, the Council voted to establish the United Nations Assistance Mission for Rwanda (UNAMIR) with an authorized strength of 5,500, but the Secretary-General found that member states were reluctant to contribute forces. As a result, UNAMIR fully deployed only after genocide had occurred, the civil war was concluded, and over a million refugees had fled the country. Poor response to the Secretary-General's appeal had multiple causes: With 17 operations already under way, traditional contributors were fatigued. The U.N. was nearly bankrupt and, therefore, tardy in reimbursing contributors. In addition, the Somalia disaster had dampened enthusiasm, especially in the United States, for ambitious operations.

## Spectrum of Peace Operations

"There are clear objectives and an understanding of where the mission fits on the spectrum between traditional peace-keeping and peace enforcement."

**Where on the Spectrum?** The Security Council should select the most appropriate operation on a spectrum extending from the low end (observation) to the high end (peace enforcement). The United States, together with other members of the Council, should make this choice on the basis of the issues presented in this report, but especially on the basis of the nature of the conflict, the consent of the parties, and the consensus for action in the Security Council.

**Will Several Operations Be Related?** Complex situations may require a series of operations or the simultaneous execution of various types of operations. In Somalia, for example, the Security Council authorized a sequence of various types of operations: security for humanitarian aid, transition, peace enforcement, and security again, marking time until U.N. forces were evacuated under U.S. protection. Each of these operations was conditioned by its predecessor—but they were not properly related. The relationship of the U.S.–led Unified Task Force (UNITAF) to the Second United Nations Operation in Somalia (UNOSOM II) was especially problematic. In the former Yugoslavia during early 1995, the Security Council simultaneously authorized three related operations: interposition in Croatia, observation in Macedonia, and peace enforcement in Bosnia-Herzegovina.

**Discontinuities.** The spectrum of peace operations is not a smooth continuum. On the contrary, it is discontinuous, meaning that the Security Council should not attempt to move across the spectrum without facing the implications of certain decisions. These include decisions to attempt "preventive deployment," invoke Chapter VII, and initiate peace enforcement.

*"Preventive Deployment."* When the Security council decides to use peace-keeping techniques to deter acts of aggression ("preventive deployment"), it indicates determination to respond promptly and forcefully if violations occur. Therefore, the Security Council or its agents must prepare such a response or else risk loss of prestige if challenged.

*Invoking Chapter VII.* Invoking Chapter VII implies willingness to coerce parties that violate their agreements or resolutions of the Security Council. Therefore, the Security Council should select a capable agent and should be certain that member states will provide adequate forces. Absent these preparations, recalcitrant parties might feel encouraged to defy the Council.

*Peace Enforcement.* When the Security Council decides to coerce a recalcitrant party, it crosses a Rubicon between noncoercive operations with continuous consent and coercive operations to impose the will of the Council. The peace force ceases to be a *noncombatant*, relying on restraint of the parties for its security, and becomes a *combatant*, relying on its own combat power for security. An attempt to mingle such radically dissimilar roles might cause the operation to degenerate into confused half-measures, as occurred in Somalia and Bosnia-Herzegovina.

## Chapter VI Peace-Keeping

"For traditional (Chapter VI) peacekeeping operations, a cease-fire should be in place and the consent of the parties obtained before the force is deployed."

Parties manifest *formal* consent when they agree to a mandate, typically including a cease-fire, separation of forces by a buffer zone, and measures to build confidence. They manifest *actual* consent by respecting the peace force and cooperating with it. Thus, actual consent may be fully apparent only after the peace operation has begun. However, it is possible to predict consent based on the previous behavior of the parties and the compatibility of their long-term goals with the mandate. To take a recent example, it would have surprised many observers if the Pol Pot faction of the Khmer Rouge had kept its promise to disarm under the Paris Agreement of 1991. See Chapter Four for issues related to consent of the parties.

## Chapter VII Peace Enforcement

"For peace enforcement (Chapter VII) operations, the threat to international peace and security is considered significant."

Actually, any type of peace operation might be launched in the face of significant threat, not only peace enforcement. For example, the Arab-Israeli wars certainly posed significant threat, yet the Security Council authorized only traditional peace-keeping operations.

## Means and Mandate

"The means to accomplish the mission are available, including the forces, financing and a mandate appropriate to the mission."

A mandate is not a means to accomplish the mission. On the contrary, it *defines* the mission, both for the peace force and for the parties. The authority to issue a mandate resides in the Security Council. The actual wording of a mandate may appear in resolutions of the Security Council, reports of the Secretary-General and his representatives, agreements of the parties, and mission statements of commanders. A mandate is appropriate if the commander can reasonably be expected to accomplish its provisions with the forces and means at his disposal. Forces and means depend upon the extent of international support, especially from the participating states. See Chapter Five for issues related to mandates and Chapter Six for issues relating to peace forces.

## Is Inaction Unacceptable?

"The political, economic and humanitarian consequences of inaction by the international community have been weighed and are considered unacceptable."

The geopolitical interests of the Permanent Five weigh heavily in a determination of what is unacceptable. For example, the Security Council responded more strongly to "ethnic cleansing" in the former Yugoslavia than to genocide in Rwanda: The former Yugoslavia attracted greater attention because of its location and historical associations with great powers. For similar reasons, the United States believed that the consequences of inaction in Haiti would be unacceptable, whereas powers farther removed felt less urgency.

## Anticipated Duration

"The operation's anticipated duration is tied to clear objectives and realistic criteria for ending the operation."

Peace operations become interminable when parties fail to reach a political settlement and the Security Council prefers to continue the operation rather than accept risks associated with termination. Examples are the United Nations Peace-Keeping Force in Cyprus and the United Nations Disengagement Observer Force (UNDOF) deployed on the Golan Heights. Even if Israel and Syria conclude a settlement, some peace-keeping force is likely to remain on the Golan Heights to assure both parties that neither is encroaching on this strategic terrain. Although interminable, these operations are also tolerable because the parties are not actively hostile and the peace force can be sustained at reasonable cost.

Accomplishing the objectives of a peace operation usually requires action from the parties. But waiting for these parties to act might make an operation interminable. As an alternative, the Security Council can simply set a time limit, putting the parties on notice that its patience is not infinite and that the parties have a limited period of time to avail themselves of assistance. Currently, mandates have limited duration, typically to a year or six months. But the Security Council renews mandates with little debate—even when the force has long failed to accomplish its mandate, as in the cases of the United Nation Interim Force in Lebanon (UNIFIL) and the United Nations Military Observer Group in India and Pakistan (UNMOGIP). For the Implementation Force (IFOR) in Bosnia-Herzegovina, the United States set an arbitrary time limit of one year.

## SHOULD THE UNITED STATES PARTICIPATE?

*Administration's Policy* distinguishes between participation in peace operations generally and those that "are likely to involve combat." Of course, all peace operations could involve combat in the sense of self-defense, but, at the high end, they could involve *combat opera-*

*tions,* meaning employment of force above the tactical level[12] to accomplish some aim beyond self-defense. The criteria outlined in *Administration's Policy* for success in operations that "are likely to involve combat" actually apply to lesser operations as well. Indeed, they lie at the heart of all soundly conceived military operations.

## Issues Concerning U.S. Participation

The following issues should be raised when deciding on U.S. participation in a peace operation:

- Are combat operations expected?
- What U.S. capabilities might be required?
- Who will be held responsible for the outcome?
- If the United States participates, would its prestige be affected?
- What U.S. interests would justify U.S. participation?

These issues are conditioned by the type of peace operation, as follows:

**Peace-Keeping to Facilitate Agreements.** Troops from many other member states can perform basic peace-keeping successfully.[13] Indeed, some traditional contributors, such as Austria, Canada, and Sweden, have greater experience in traditional peace-keeping than does the United States. But certain U.S. capabilities might be crucial to success, especially global airlift and sealift, and intelligence collection. Because parties are solely responsible for maintaining their agreements, U.S. prestige would not be at risk if the United States chose to participate. Its participation might be justified by a broad, enduring interest in international peace and security.

---

[12]The *tactical level* involves engagements and even battles of limited duration. In the context of peace operations, returning hostile fire would be a typical action at the tactical level; long-term protection of a safe area would be at the operational level.

[13]See Chapter Three, "Evaluating the Problems and Potential of Non–U.S. Forces," in Preston Niblack, Thomas S. Szayna, and John Bordeaux, *Increasing the Availability and Effectiveness of Non–U.S. Forces for Peace Operations,* RAND, Santa Monica, Calif., MR-701-OSD, 1996.

**Peace-Keeping to Deter Violations.** The tasks associated with "preventive deployment" are identical to those of traditional peace-keeping; therefore, other member states can usually contribute qualified troops. But the United States might choose to participate in order to demonstrate its commitment to respond if violations occur and perhaps also to prepare its response. Currently, the United States is the foremost contributor to UNPREDEP, which is deployed on the northern border of the former Yugoslav Republic of Macedonia. This participation implies U.S. commitment to respond to border violations, consonant with a U.S. diplomatic warning to Yugoslavia (Serbia and Montenegro). UNPREDEP is designed to observe the border, not to defend it, and therefore another force would be required to respond forcefully. In such a contingency, the United States would become responsible for the outcome and its prestige *would be* involved.

**U.S. Participation in More-Ambitious Operations (VI).** More-ambitious operations under Chapter VI often require capabilities lacking in many member states, especially strategic mobility, intelligence collection, logistics support, and civic action to repair and replace damaged infrastructure. Therefore, U.S. participation might be extremely helpful or even required for success. When the United States participates in such operations, its prestige is engaged, but only to a limited extent. Responsibility rests primarily on the parties or, in the absence of parties, on populations and new governments. At most, the Security Council and participating member states might be criticized for expending disproportionate resources on an ill-defined or unrealistic peace operation.

**U.S. Participation in More-Ambitious Operations (VII).** By invoking Chapter VII, the Security Council expresses its willingness to employ force, potentially to coerce parties. Therefore, the peace force must be ready to conduct combat operations. The forces of many member states are unskilled in providing security to a civilian population, have little experience in combined arms, and generate only limited combat power; therefore, U.S. participation will often be required to ensure success. When the United States participates in ambitious operations under Chapter VII—which might include urgent humanitarian concern, concern for regional stability, and specific geopolitical interests—its prestige will be affected by the outcome and its interests should justify this exposure.

**U.S. Participation in Peace Enforcement.** If combat operations become necessary, U.S. capabilities will usually be required for success, even when other great powers also participate. Required U.S. capabilities may include global airlift and sealift, transportation within the region, intelligence at every level, fire support, forced entry, special operations, and expertise in combined arms. The outcome of any combat operation in which the United States participates will affect its prestige. Regional opponents will probably evaluate U.S. will and capabilities by its performance in peace enforcement. When the United States chooses to participate, its specific geopolitical interests should justify combat operations on the scale required to accomplish the mandate. Absent such interests, U.S. domestic opinion is unlikely to support the attendant expense and casualties.

## Summary of Issues Concerning U.S. Participation

Figure 2.1 summarizes issues concerning U.S. participation within a simplified framework of peace operations.

RAND*MR583-2.1*

| | Peace-Keeping to Facilitate Agreements | Peace-Keeping to Deter Violations | More-Ambitious Operations Under Chapter VI | More-Ambitious Operations Under Chapter VII | Peace Enforcement |
|---|---|---|---|---|---|
| Are Combat Operations Required? | No | Potentially in response to violations[a] | No | Potentially | Yes |
| What U.S. Capabilities Might Be Required? | Strategic mobility, intelligence collection | Presence to demonstrate commitment and prepare response | Strategic mobility, intelligence, logistics support, civic action | U.S. leadership and control, forced entry, combined arms | U.S. leadership and control, forced entry, combined arms |
| Who Will Be Held Responsible for the Outcome? | Parties to the conflict are solely responsible | 1. Violators 2. UNSC and member states for their response | 1. Parties 2. Populations and new governments | 1. Parties 2. UNSC and member states | UNSC and participating member states |
| If U.S. Participates, Would Its Global Prestige Be Affected? | No | Yes | To a limited extent | Yes | Yes |
| What U.S. Interests Would Justify Participation? | Concern for international peace and security | Concern for regional stability, special strategic concern, treaty commitment | Urgent humanitarian concern, concern for regional stability, etc. | Urgent humanitarian concern, geopolitical interests | Geopolitical interests |

[a]Response to violations normally requires additional forces.

**Figure 2.1—Issues Concerning U.S. Participation**

As the Security Council ascends from peace-keeping to peace enforcement, it assumes increasing responsibility for outcomes.  At the
low end (peace-keeping to facilitate agreements), the parties bear
sole responsibility for keeping agreements concluded in their own
interests.  The Security Council offers help in implementing those
agreements but does not accept responsibility.  At the high end of the
spectrum (peace enforcement), the Security Council assumes full responsibility.  Representing the world community, it cannot claim to
lack resources and must ascribe any failure to inadequate consensus
or to lack of determination among its members.  Similarly, when the
United States chooses to participate, it will increasingly be held responsible and its national prestige will increasingly be affected as it
ascends from peace-keeping to peace enforcement.

# Chapter Three

# NATURE OF THE CONFLICT

How amenable is the conflict to peace operations? Peace operations are limited applications of military force, rarely if ever decisive in themselves. Their chances of success depend heavily upon whether the conflict has characteristics that make it amenable or intractable. Among the important considerations are stage of the conflict, presence of unconventional warfare, aims of parties, degree of control over combatants, and inherent risk to personnel participating in the operation.

## STAGE OF THE CONFLICT

Once fighting has broken out, a conflict may not be amenable to peace operations until culmination or stalemate is reached. *Culmination* is reached when the stronger party has attained important aims and cannot attain more through force. *Stalemate* occurs when the parties countervail so that no party is likely to attain its aims through force. The major Arab-Israeli wars[1] culminated when Israel had won campaigns that attained certain strategic goals, but could not proceed further because its resources were limited and great powers exerted pressure to contain the conflict. Culmination is usually more propitious for peace operations than stalemate, because parties are reluctant to concede that stalemate cannot be over-

---

[1] First Arab-Israeli War (1948–1949), Sinai War (1956), Six Day War (1967), Yom Kippur War (1973).

come.[2]  For several years, the conflict in Bosnia-Herzegovina was largely stalemated, yet the Bosnian Serbs resisted a peace settlement until Croats made gains that jarred their confidence.  The parties in Angola fought for two decades and finally reached agreement only after the Luandan government gained the upper hand.

The conflict in southern Lebanon has been stalemated for over a decade, yet still is not amenable to peace operations.  Syria helps Iran to arm Hezbollah in order to pressure Israel into making concessions on other issues, especially the Golan Heights.  Israel continues to believe that it needs a security zone in southern Lebanon to secure its people from terrorist attack.  In May 1995, Israel conducted a heavy bombardment that inflicted considerable suffering on the Lebanese people, yet still failed to make the Lebanese government curtail Hezbollah's military activities.  UNIFIL is deployed partly within the Israeli security zone and partly north of it, literally caught in the middle of this complex conflict.

From their various perspectives, parties often assess conflicts differently.  From the Turkish Cypriot perspective, the conflict in Cyprus culminated in 1974 with partition between the two communities; but from the Greek Cypriot perspective, the conflict is only stalemated.  From the Bosnian Serb perspective, the 1991 war between Croatia and Yugoslavia culminated in de facto independence for Krajina, whereas Croatia recognized only a momentary stalemate that it eventually overcame with military force.

## PREVALENCE OF UNCONVENTIONAL WARFARE

*Unconventional warfare* involves irregular forces employing raiding tactics.  There may be no lines of confrontation or combatants may operate extensively behind the lines of confrontation.  The distinction between *combatants* and *noncombatants* may be obscured to

---

[2]"If neither side manages to pound the other into submission and a stalemate emerges, does a compromise peace become more practical?  Not for a long time, and not until many more lives have been invested in the contending quests for victory.  Stalemates rarely seem solid to those with a strong stake in overcoming them."  Richard K. Betts, "The Delusion of Impartial Intervention," *Foreign Affairs*, November/December 1994, pp. 23–24.

the point that it becomes meaningless. Under such circumstances, peace operations may be severely hampered or unworkable.

The techniques of traditional peace-keeping are particularly ill-suited to handling unconventional warfare. Military observers are ineffective at monitoring the activities of irregular forces, such as the mujahideen in Afghanistan, forces of the Palestine Liberation Organization (PLO) in Lebanon, or Contras in Central America, because such forces operate in unpredictable ways and may not even be identifiable as combatants. Interposition requires that conventional forces disengage from the line of confrontation where the buffer zone will be established. This technique is ineffective or senseless if irregular forces are scattered throughout the country or can easily infiltrate the buffer zone. For example, interposition is unworkable in southern Lebanon, where parties are intermingled; almost any male is a potential combatant, and ambushes are a favorite tactic.

## IRRECONCILABLE AIMS AND ANIMOSITY

Parties have opposing aims, and they seek to realize those aims through force or threat of force. As an outcome of conflict, they may abandon or modify their aims until those aims become compatible, or they may continue to have irreconcilable aims. *Irreconcilable aims* imply that the conflict is still basically unresolved; they threaten the ultimate success of a peace operation.

The tenacity with which parties hold to particular aims frequently is affected by the level of animosity that has built up between them. Animosity normally accompanies conflict. When it becomes especially visceral, it makes some types of peace operations unworkable, especially those that require the parties to cooperate with each other. Virulent animosity often occurs among tribes or nationalities that are intermingled and competing for the same territory.

Transition operations are especially sensitive to the level of animosity. In Cyprus, for example, Orthodox Christian Cypriots of Greek extraction and Moslem Cypriots of Turkish extraction fell into an irregular civil war during 1963. The United Nations Peace-Keeping

Force in Cyprus received a mandate to facilitate a return to "normal conditions,"[3] implying restoration of a single government. But mutual animosity was so great that Turkish Cypriots refused to participate in the Republic of Cyprus, fearing discrimination as a minority. As a result, UNFICYP could not restore "normal conditions," although it did much to allay tensions prior to the Turkish intervention of 1974.

## DEGREE OF CONTROL OVER COMBATANTS

So long as the parties maintain their consent, conflict is more amenable to peace operations if the parties exert strong control over combatants. If the parties lose control, then peace operations are hampered because the issue of responsibility for disruptive actions is blurred.

Implicit in peace-keeping is an expectation that the parties will implement their agreements, based on a presumption that they control their adherents. Absent such control, there is little point in monitoring activity for which no party will accept responsibility. For example, the United Nations Good Offices Mission in Afghanistan and Pakistan had a mandate to monitor compliance with the Geneva Accords of 1988, requiring, among other things, that Afghanistan and Pakistan not interfere in each others' internal affairs. The observers duly recorded over 7,000 complaints from Afghanistan and over 1,000 complaints from Pakistan; however, they were unable to resolve them, partly because of unsettled conditions, especially in an Afghanistan dominated by armed bands with local allegiances.

In contrast, control was seldom an issue during peace operations in the Sinai and on the Golan Heights. The parties firmly controlled their forces and could be held accountable for violations of the cease-fires or intrusion into the buffer zones.

---

[3]Officially, UNFICYP still has the mandate contained in Resolution 186, adopted on March 4, 1964: "to use its best efforts to prevent a recurrence of fighting and, as necessary, to contribute to the maintenance and restoration of law and order and a return to normal conditions." But since the Turkish intervention, UNFICYP has acted primarily as an interposition force, stabilizing a de facto partition of the island.

More-ambitious peace operations also assume that the parties will cooperate to accomplish the mandate. But cooperation becomes ineffective if the parties cannot control their adherents or if significant groups are left outside the peace process. In addition, unscrupulous parties may deny responsibility for their deliberate acts. For example, the United Nations Transitional Authority in Cambodia (UNTAC) had a mandate to supervise and control administration in Cambodia until a new Cambodian government had been created. But in 1992–1993, Cambodia was plagued by widespread banditry, which could not be suppressed by a corrupt and inefficient government. UNTAC lost popularity with the Cambodian people because it was largely unable to make their lives more secure.

As another example, the United Nations Protection Force[4] had a mandate to demilitarize and protect certain Serb-held areas of Croatia, especially Krajina. But in 1992, Krajina was rife with irregular bands and local militias, whose activities could be disavowed by the Serb authorities in Knin. Lack of central control, coupled with duplicity, frustrated attempts to carry out the mandate.

## RISK TO PERSONNEL

All peace operations involve some risk to personnel, both military and civilian. The acceptable level of risk varies according to the type of operation and the level of international support.

Peace-keeping normally entails low risk to personnel; indeed, high casualties would invalidate the very concept. For example, the most dangerous observer mission to date has been the United Nations Truce Supervision Organization (UNTSO) in the Near East. Since its inception in 1948, UNTSO has suffered 28 fatalities.[5]

---

[4]UNPROFOR operations in Croatia were redesignated the United Nations Confidence Restoration Operation in Croatia (UNCRO) in early 1995. President Franjo Tudjman of Croatia demanded the addition of "in Croatia" to the name to buttress the Croatian claim to sovereignty over Krajina.

[5]The most dangerous period was during 1948–1949, when approximately 500 United Nations personnel attempted to monitor cease-fires among Jews, Palestinians, and other Arab forces. Lack of agreement on the demarcation lines, numerous cease-fire violations, and incidents of terrorism contributed to the risk. The United Nations Mediator, Count Bernadotte of Sweden, and a senior French military observer were assassinated in 1948 by a Jewish terrorist organization.

Risk to forces interposing themselves between the parties is usually high during the initial disengagement, then declines to an uneventful routine.  For example, interposition was risky on Cyprus during the Turkish intervention in 1974, but became a comfortable routine in subsequent years.

Participating states must expect casualties during operations conducted under Chapter VII.  For example, about 140 United Nations personnel were killed during peace operations in Somalia.  Of those, 92 were considered killed in action, 41 of them from the United States, including 18 killed in the action on October 3, 1993.

The Security Council might reduce the likelihood of combat by deploying a powerful force that parties would fear to challenge, such as UNITAF[6] in Somalia.  But such forces will seldom be available. Almost invariably, the peace force has been too weak to deter confrontation, even in the largest peace operations, including Cambodia, Croatia, Bosnia-Herzegovina during UNPROFOR, and Somalia during UNOSOM II.

Understandably, governments are less tolerant of casualties in peace operations than during operations conducted unilaterally for reasons of national policy.  Therefore, the Security Council or its agents have tended to reduce risk by dropping provisions of the mandate or deciding to conduct a different type of operation.

------

[6]The name UNITAF was chosen to express the multilateral character of the force. UNITAF existed from December 9, 1992, through May 4, 1993, when it relinquished responsibility to UNOSOM II.  In U.S. terminology, the UNITAF period corresponded to Operation Restore Hope.

# Chapter Four

# CONSENT OF THE PARTIES

How willing are the parties to help accomplish the mandate? *Consent* is the evident willingness of parties to help accomplish a mandate. *Formal* consent is manifested in statements, declarations, accords, agreements, and treaties. *Actual* consent becomes apparent from the behavior of the parties in the course of a peace operation. Therefore, consent cannot be known with certainty until the operation is under way.

Consent is central to all peace operations, including peace enforcement, which may start when consent is lost. To understand the effect of consent on an operation, the Security Council needs to consider how much consent is required, its current status, the prospects for maintaining it, and, finally, how the Council intends to respond if parties withdraw their consent. All of these issues are sensitive to the type of operation that is contemplated or under way and have to be considered in that context. For example, the parties in Cyprus rejected a transition mandate, which would have restored a common government, because they so mistrusted each other, but they consented to interposition.

## PEACE-KEEPING

### Observation to Facilitate Agreements

Observers monitor the parties' compliance with agreements, report violations, and often mediate among the parties.

**Required Consent.**  How much consent is required from the parties to ensure accomplishment of the mandate?  What security arrangements should the parties make?  What information should the parties provide to the observers?  How much freedom of movement will observers need?  What vehicles, surveillance devices, and communications equipment should the observers be allowed to operate?  What immunities should be enjoyed by indigenous employees of the observation force?

Consent always implies freedom of movement for the observers and often specifies the types of equipment observers will be allowed to use.  For example, Iran never fully consented to operations of the United Nations Iran-Iraq Military Observer Group (UNIIMOG).  In contrast to the Iraqi side, Iran severely hampered the observers' freedom of movement.  It refused to allow UNIIMOG to operate helicopters in its airspace and initially prohibited use of radio-equipped vehicles.  It harassed Iranian nationals employed by UNIIMOG and prohibited them from crossing the border into Iraq in the course of their duties.

**Current Consent.**  Does consent currently appear adequate?  How strongly are the parties committed to maintaining their agreements?  How do they assess the current balance of military power?  How are they affected by political pressure from great powers or from regional powers?  In their response to intervening events, have the parties shown a good-faith commitment to their agreements?

Parties sometimes accept an observation mission to obtain a respite from fighting or to avoid the opprobrium of appearing intransigent, although they do not fully support the peace process.  In such circumstances, observation may serve little purpose.  For example, in 1962 the Kennedy Administration pressed Egypt and Saudi Arabia to disengage from the civil war raging in Yemen between Republicans and Royalists.  Neither Egypt nor Saudi Arabia wished to appear unreasonable.  Moreover, each had its own reasons for wanting to disengage: Egypt feared that its forces had become overextended; Saudi Arabia wanted to inhibit an Egyptian-supported advance north of the Yemen border.  But both Egypt and Saudi Arabia continued to support opposite sides in an unresolved civil war; therefore, they did not fully cooperate with the United Nations Yemen Observation Mission (UNYOM).

**Prospects for Consent.**  What are the prospects for maintaining adequate consent?  The propensity for parties to withdraw consent depends on the compatibility of the mandate with their long-term aims.  What are those aims?  What political, economic, or military developments would be likely to affect the parties' chances of achieving those aims?  What activities would the parties wish to conceal from impartial observers?  The prospect for consent is also affected by the parties' perceptions of the impartiality of the observer force.  What kind of developments or behavior on the part of the observers would be likely to make them appear partial?

A party is likely to withdraw consent when it wishes to exploit a favorable military situation or to conceal activities that might be politically embarrassing.  For example, India withdrew its consent to the United Nations Military Observer Group in India and Pakistan, whose mandate was to oversee the 1949 cease-fire in Kashmir.  When war broke out again in 1971, Indian forces advanced beyond the 1949 cease-fire line and subsequently waged a protracted counterinsurgency campaign against Muslim opposition in Kashmir.  India thus had two motives for withdrawing consent:  desire to retain territory gained in 1971 and unwillingness to subject Indian counterinsurgency efforts to scrutiny.

**Response to Withdrawal of Consent.**  What responses should be planned in the event one or more parties withdraw consent?  Should the Security Council terminate the mandate?  Should it persevere, even if there is little prospect of success?  Should it alter the mandate to fit new circumstances?

Parties demonstrate their lack of consent by refusing to cooperate with the observer force or by violating agreements so egregiously that observation ceases to be worthwhile.  In some cases, the Security Council has simply terminated the mandate—for example, the United Nations Yemen Observation Force.  In other cases, the Security Council has persevered without much prospect of success.  For example, the United Nations Military Observer Group in India and Pakistan is still in place, although India has not cooperated since 1971.

Alternatively, the U.N. might elect to leave a diplomatic mission after the observers depart.  For example, in place of the United Nations

Good Offices Mission in Afghanistan and Pakistan, the Secretary-General established the Office of the Secretary-General in Afghanistan and Pakistan to mediate agreements among the various factions.

In Angola, the Security Council allowed a failing operation to continue at reduced strength until new developments allowed a more ambitious operation.    The Second United Nations Angola Verification Mission (UNAVEM II)[1] was established to monitor a peace agreement between the Angolan government and *União Nacional para a Independência Total de Angola* (UNITA).  But during 1992, UNITA refused to accept its defeat in national elections and withdrew from the peace process, precipitating yet another round in a civil war that had begun in the early 1970s.  Reduced to 50 military personnel, UNAVEM II kept an eye on the war and assisted in the delivery of humanitarian aid.  On November 20, 1994, under U.N. mediation, the parties signed the Lusaka Protocol, which envisioned national reconciliation, with certain government positions reserved for the UNITA leadership.  Fighting continued after signature of the Protocol but began to subside after a successful government offensive.  In February 1995, the Security Council established UNAVEM III with an ambitious mandate to assist in achieving national reconciliation.[2]  By early 1996, little progress had been made in the cantonment of UNITA troops, much less their integration into a national army; yet it appeared that the long-protracted civil war might finally be winding down because UNITA was becoming fatigued.

---

[1]Although UNAVEM I merged into UNAVEM II, these two operations had very different mandates.  UNAVEM I was mandated to oversee withdrawal of foreign troops; UNAVEM II was concerned with the Angolan civil war.  In December 1988, UNAVEM I was established to verify withdrawal of Cuban troops from Angola as part of a broader settlement that ensured creation of an independent Namibia.  The last Cubans departed ahead of schedule, during May 1991.  *Acordos de Paz para Angola,* signed in Lisbon under Portuguese mediation on May 31, included a cease-fire, followed by national elections, and integration of Government forces and UNITA into a single national army.  UNAVEM II was mandated to facilitate implementation of *Acordos de Paz.*

[2]Security Council Resolution 976 on February 8, 1995, authorized establishment of UNAVEM III with a strength of 7,000 military personnel "to assist the parties in restoring peace and achieving national reconciliation in Angola under the *Acordos de Paz,* the Lusaka Protocol and relevant Security Council resolutions."  UNAVEM III was thus directed to monitor disarmament and demobilization, and to facilitate integration of UNITA into police, army, and government—an ambitious transition mandate.

## Observation to Deter Violations

The Security Council deploys observers with the intention of deterring parties from violating their agreements and international law. Observers symbolize the Security Council's will to respond if violations occur. The parties must believe that the Security Council will respond, because it is this belief that deters violations.

## Interposition to Facilitate Agreements

The peace force interposes itself between the parties by controlling a buffer zone. The intention of the Security Council is to facilitate agreements among the parties, especially on disengagement of forces and related arms limitations, by assuring each party that others are complying or making efforts to comply. The interposed force has usually been lightly armed and is able to control the buffer zone, but is not able to defeat large-scale incursion.[3]

**Required Consent.** How much consent is required from the parties? Interposition requires the parties to relinquish control over the buffer zone to the peace force. In addition, the parties may agree to arms limitations in contiguous territory and to other confidence-building measures.

How much freedom of movement should the parties accord to the peace force so that it can accomplish its mandate? What logistics support should the parties provide? To what extent must the parties surrender the functions of government within the buffer zone? What curtailment of border control and customs should the parties accept? What information concerning their forces should the parties provide? What restrictions on deployment of their forces outside the buffer zone should the parties accept? What formal arrangements are required to resolve incidents and to resolve disputes concerning the interpretation of agreements?

---

[3]The Implementation Force is an exception, because it includes armor, artillery, attack helicopters, and on-call close air support sufficient to enforce—not merely to control—a buffer zone between two entities in Bosnia-Herzegovina (Croat-Muslim Federation and Serb Republic). However, IFOR operates in the context of a more ambitious transition operation as set forth in the Dayton Agreements.

In 1974, the United Nations Peace-Keeping Force in Cyprus interposed itself between Greek Cypriot forces and invading Turkish forces. Following a cease-fire on August 16, 1974, through many agreements with local military commanders, UNFICYP recorded the line of confrontation and established the buffer zone. Although consenting to UNFICYP's control over a buffer zone, the parties have not allowed peace-keepers to move freely outside the zone. An incipient arms race appears to be increasing the tension in Cyprus.[4] It might be allayed if UNFICYP were allowed to inspect and report on armaments throughout the island. But the parties have refused to grant UNFICYP such powers and adequate freedom of movement.

**Current Consent.** Does consent currently appear adequate? Parties expect that interposition will tend to fix the line of confrontation, and they are usually willing to accept that outcome, at least for the time being, when they give consent. Largely for this reason, interposition has been the most consistently successful type of peace operation.

Consent may depend on calculations of relative advantage in a complex political-military situation. An interesting example is the Second United Nations Emergency Force (UNEF II), established to control a buffer between Egyptian and Israeli forces at the conclusion of the 1973 Arab-Israeli War (also known as the Yom Kippur War). Anxious to avoid confrontation among themselves, the United States and the Soviet Union persuaded their allies to disengage forces and to accept interposition. Egypt agreed because its forces had suffered defeat and little outside help was in sight. Israel agreed because it realized that it would not be allowed to starve out the Egyptian Third Army and that Israeli forces could not remain west of the Suez Canal indefinitely.

---

[4]Turkey maintains the strongest force in Cyprus, a corps of 30,000 men equipped with 265 A5 M-48 main battle tanks, over 100 armored personnel carriers, and nearly 200 pieces of artillery. Although far weaker, the Cypriot National Guard has embarked on an extensive program of modernization. During 1995, it increased its holdings of AMX-30B main battle tanks from 52 to 104 and took delivery of 18 BMP-3 infantry fighting vehicles. In addition, the National Guard improved its fortifications along the buffer zone. In December 1995, Secretary-General Boutros-Ghali expressed "serious concern at the excessive levels of military forces and armaments in Cyprus and at the rate at which these are being strengthened." United Nations, *Report of the Secretary-General on the United Nations Operation in Cyprus*, S/1995/1020, December 10, 1995.

**Prospects for Consent.** What are the prospects for maintaining adequate consent? If the parties have long-term objectives that are incompatible with fixing the line of confrontation, they may accept interposition as a respite and renew hostilities when they sense an advantage. How compatible is interposition with the long-term objectives of the parties? What political or military developments would cause a party to renew hostilities? How does political pressure from great powers or from regional powers affect the willingness of parties to observe provisions of the interposition mandate?

Conflict between Croatia and the Croatian (Krajina) Serbs offers an example. After several cease-fires and renewed hostilities, Croatia agreed in early 1994 to a buffer zone between its forces and the Croatian Serbs that would be controlled by UNPROFOR.[5] The Krajina Serbs were amenable to interposition, because it contributed to their security and tended to confirm their separation from Zagreb. But interposition ran counter to Zagreb's long-term objective to reassert its authority over Krajina. After repeatedly threatening to withdraw his consent, President Franjo Tudjman of Croatia announced on March 12, 1995, that he would consent to a new mandate that included observation of the Bosnian-Croatian border. At the same time, UNPROFOR was to be renamed the United Nations Confidence Restoration Operation in Croatia (UNCRO) and reduced in size.

On May 1, 1995, the Croatian Army launched a well-prepared combined-arms offensive that quickly overran the Serb-held part of Sector West (Western Slavonia), brushing aside UNCRO forces. Then, on August 4, the Croatian Army advanced into Krajina, overrunning UNCRO observation posts and compelling the Serb inhabitants to flee. Three UNCRO soldiers were killed, and several were forced to serve as human shields. The Security Council deplored these actions but made no forceful response, in part because the

---

[5]Achieved through the good offices of the United States and Russia, this agreement was concluded on March 30, 1994, at the Russian Embassy in Zagreb. Croatia and the Krajina Serbs agreed to withdraw their forces 1 kilometer from a 370-kilometer-long line of confrontation. In addition, they agreed to move heavy weapons 10 kilometers away from the line. The agreement included approval of 34 maps describing the line of confrontation. Pursuant to this agreement, UNPROFOR established observation posts and checkpoints to control the buffer zone.

United States had tacitly approved this offensive.[6]  Interposition had failed because it ran counter to a fundamental long-term objective of the stronger party.

**Response to Withdrawal of Consent.**  What response should be planned in the event one or more parties withdraw consent?  How should the Security Council respond to a demand from either party for the force to withdraw?  How should the Security Council respond if parties violate the buffer zone?  What actions should the peace force take?

If a party withdraws consent, the Security Council might decide to withdraw the peace force, to change its mandate, or to protest the renewal of hostilities.  For example, on May 16, 1967, Egypt demanded that the First United Nations Emergency Force relinquish certain observation posts in the Sinai.  Since Israel refused to allow deployment of the force on its side of the line of confrontation, Secretary-General U Thant saw no alternative but to order that UNEF I withdraw completely.  On June 5, Israel launched a preemptive strike against Egypt that opened the Six Day War.  Unable to complete their withdrawal in time, 15 UNEF I soldiers were killed in crossfire.

### Interposition to Deter Violations

The peace force occupies a buffer zone, often along an international border, to deter parties from violations.  It performs a symbolic function of demonstrating the Security Council's will to respond if violations occur.  The United Nations Iraq-Kuwait Observer Mission has this mandate (despite its name), because it is expected to control a buffer zone along the Kuwaiti-Iraqi border, which was established after the Persian Gulf War.  A critical issue is the parties' belief that the United States will respond to violations, since this belief is what ensures deterrence.

---

[6]Dana Priest, "U.S. Cautiously Supports Offensive Against Serbs," *Washington Post*, August 5, 1995, p. A14; Ann Devroy, "Croatian Victory Creates Opportunity to Broker Bosnian Peace, Clinton Says," *Washington Post*, August 8, 1995, p. A15.

## MORE-AMBITIOUS OPERATIONS

### Transition

The peace force helps facilitate change in the status and condition of a country under Chapter VI, or it compels parties to effect such change under Chapter VII.

**Required Consent.** How much consent is required from the parties? Consent to a transition operation requires the parties' willingness to cooperate actively with the peace force, often by implementing highly detailed agreements with implications for governmental structure, military forces, reconstruction, and economic recovery.

For example, the Agreement on a Comprehensive Political Settlement of the Cambodia Conflict, signed on October 23, 1991, in Paris, contained highly detailed provisions for a transition from civil war to a new national government through the presence of the United Nations Transitional Authority in Cambodia. Among other provisions, it described creation of a Supreme National Council, which would include representatives from each of the Cambodian factions. In a formal sense, the parties gave their consent when their representatives signed this agreement.

In another example, the warring factions in Somalia concluded a General Agreement on January 15, 1993, that foresaw control of heavy weapons by an international authority, disarmament of militias in cantonments, and immediate disarmament of other armed elements, including bandits. On March 27, the factions concluded a more comprehensive agreement, which included establishment of a Transitional National Council with representatives from 15 "political movements" (factions). These agreements defined the scope of the parties' consent to operations by UNITAF and, more important, by UNOSOM II.

**Current Consent.** Does consent currently appear adequate? Do the parties appear to be acting in good faith? Conversely, are there grounds to suspect that the parties have hidden agendas? Can they firmly control their supporters? Does the current balance of local political and military power encourage or discourage the parties' consent? How does political pressure from great powers or regional powers affect their consent?

Parties may consent for tactical reasons, without fully supporting the mandate. For example, Morocco has agreed to hold a referendum on the future of Western Sahara, but its actions over the past two decades have indicated that Morocco would not accept an unfavorable outcome. In 1975, after the International Court of Justice ruled that popular will, not Morocco's historical claims, should govern, King Hassan of Morocco ordered thousands of Moroccans to enter the disputed territory.

During the late 1970s, Morocco defeated *Frente Popular para la Liberación de Saguia el-Hamra y de Rio de Oro* (POLISARIO) insurgents, who sought refuge in Algeria and switched to guerrilla tactics. From 1980 to 1987, Morocco built a 3,300-kilometer-long sand berm with interconnected forts, extending the entire length of Western Sahara. After a series of meetings mediated by the Secretary-General, Morocco and POLISARIO agreed in August 1988 to conduct a referendum under U.N. supervision. The United Nations Mission for the Referendum in Western Sahara (MINURSO) was authorized to oversee identification of voters, help conduct the referendum, and monitor withdrawal of forces in accordance with its results. But up to the current time, Morocco and POLISARIO are so far from agreement on identifying voters that the prospect of holding any referendum is remote.[7]

**Prospects for Consent.** What are the prospects for maintaining adequate consent? How compatible is the mandate with the underlying interests of the parties? What does past behavior suggest about the parties' sincerity? What developments or events would cause the

---

[7]Morocco maintains that 100,000 persons currently residing in Morocco should be allowed to apply. POLISARIO contends that the 1974 Spanish census should form the basis for identifying voters and dismisses the 100,000 applications from persons living in Morocco. In late 1995, reflecting impatience in the Security Council, the Secretary-General warned that if progress were not made, he would frame other options, including withdrawal of MINURSO. United Nations, *The Situation Concerning Western Sahara: Report of the Secretary-General*, S/1995/779, September 8, 1995. During January 1996, a Special Envoy held discussions with authorities in Morocco, Tindouf (POLISARIO), Algeria, and Mauritania. Morocco and POLISARIO both claimed that they could make no further concessions, making it doubtful that the process of identifying voters could ever be completed. But Algerian and Mauritanian authorities strongly urged that MINURSO not be withdrawn. United Nations, *Report of the Secretary-General on the Situation Concerning Western Sahara*, S/1996/43, January 19, 1996.

parties to reconsider and perhaps withdraw consent? Are there other disaffected groups that have the potential for disrupting the transition process? If outside pressure from great powers or regional powers has been instrumental in securing consent of the parties, is this pressure likely to be sustained?

Parties are seldom affected equally by the provisions of an agreement, and they are likely to withdraw consent to provisions that run strongly counter to their interests. Previous behavior will usually enable these interests to be assessed somewhat. In Cambodia, for example, one of the parties to the Paris Agreement was the Party of Democratic Kampuchea (PDK), better known as the Pol Pot faction of the Khmer Rouge. Some 15 years earlier, the Khmer Rouge massacred over 1 million Cambodians, mostly better-educated urban dwellers, in one of the century's worst political crimes. During Phase Two of the Cambodian peace process, the parties were expected to deploy their forces to cantonments, where at least 70 percent would be demobilized in preparation for national elections. But the PDK refused to disarm,[8] doubtless because it had little interest in an election it did not expect to win.

**Response to Withdrawal of Consent.** What responses should be planned if one or more parties withdraw consent? When a party refuses to cooperate, the Security Council might try to coerce it through sanctions or by authorizing peace enforcement. Alternatively, the Council might promote negotiations among the parties, change to a less intrusive mandate, or terminate the operation.

Would fresh negotiations be fruitful? What actions by the peace force or outside pressures might convince recalcitrant parties to rejoin the peace process? Should the Security Council authorize a less

---

[8]UNTAC established cantonments where FUNCINPEC (the United Front for an Independent, Neutral, Peaceful, and Cooperative Cambodia) and the Khmer People's National Liberation Front (an alliance based on the former Lon Nol regime) were disarmed. Because the PDK refused to participate, the government also evaded disarmament, although nominally continuing its support. In all, UNTAC collected 50,000 weapons through the cantonment system, a small fraction of the arms available in Cambodia. For an official perspective on this issue, see United Nations, *The United Nations and Cambodia 1991–1995,* Department of Public Information, New York, 1995, pp. 22–27.

intrusive mandate? What costs and risks would be incurred if the peace force withdraws?

In Cambodia during November 1992, the Security Council responded to the PDK's withdrawal of consent by applying economic sanctions. Resolution 792 placed export restrictions on raw materials, especially lumber and gems. This measure was intended to apply pressure on the PDK by limiting its sources of income. In Somalia during June 1992, the Council responded to an attack on UNOSOM II by authorizing peace enforcement. Resolution 837 invoked Chapter VII and reaffirmed that the Secretary-General was authorized to take "all necessary measures against those responsible for the armed attacks."

In Lebanon, the Security Council tacitly changed to a less intrusive mandate. The initial mandate for the United Nations Interim Force in Lebanon was to confirm the withdrawal of Israeli forces and to ensure resumption of control by the government of Lebanon. Unable to accomplish this transition, UNIFIL redefined its mandate as security for humanitarian aid. It provided water, food, fuel, and electricity to the civilian population. It made medical services available, and it offered some degree of physical protection to civilians in its battalion sectors.[9]

## Security for Humanitarian Aid

The peace force secures provision of humanitarian aid to persons suffering as a result of conflict or natural disaster accompanied by a collapse of civilian authority. This type of operation should be conducted under Chapter VII,[10] because security for humanitarian aid

---

[9]Mona Ghali, "United Nations Interim Force in Lebanon, 1978–Present," in William J. Durch, ed., *The Evolution of UN Peace-Keeping: Case Studies and Comparative Analysis*, St. Martin's Press, New York, 1993, pp. 199–200.

[10]The Security Council invoked Chapter VII for UNITAF in Somalia, charged with securing humanitarian aid as its primary mission, and for UNPROFOR in Bosnia-Herzegovina, charged with securing humanitarian aid in the context of a more ambitious mandate. It also invoked Chapter VII when authorizing France to carry out Operation Turquoise, an operation intended to establish a humanitarian security zone in Rwanda. Resolution 829 on June 22, 1994, welcomed the offer of member states (primarily France) to conduct an operation under national control to contribute to the security of civilians at risk in Rwanda and authorized under Chapter VII "all necessary means to achieve the humanitarian objectives."

goes beyond self-defense; however, in practice, the Security Council has invoked both Chapter VI and Chapter VII. In authorizing security for humanitarian aid, the Security Council evinces a desire to alleviate human suffering but is also reluctant to become involved in the underlying conflict.

**Required Consent.** How much consent is required from the parties? What freedom of movement will the peace force require? What airports and seaports should be made available to the peace force? What other facilities, such as warehouses and depots, should be made available? What privileges and immunities should be enjoyed by non-governmental organizations and their employees? What support should be provided by the parties to the conflict?

*Consent* implies that the parties agree to respect the peace force and not interfere with provision of humanitarian aid, typically including its delivery, storage, transportation, administration, and distribution. In most cases, NGOs are already present in the area when the Security Council authorizes these operations; therefore, consent applies to their activities as well.

For example, the United Nations Assistance Mission in Rwanda had consent to operate within Rwanda—but not in neighboring Zaire and Tanzania, where Hutu refugees fled from advancing Tutsi forces. As a result, elements of the Hutu government and army were able to establish unchallenged control over the refugee camps. By late 1994, through murder and intimidation, these elements controlled all aspects of life in the camps, including distribution of humanitarian aid.[11]

**Current Consent.** Does consent currently appear adequate? Do the parties appear willing to allow the aid to reach all the intended recipients? Do they firmly control their supporters? Do elements other than the parties, such as bandits and armed gangs, threaten humanitarian aid?

---

[11]Beginning in February 1995, the U.N. paid for 1,500 Zairian troops to keep order in the refugee camps around Goma. This was the first time in U.N. history that a country's troops were authorized to conduct peace operations on their own national territory.

**Prospects for Consent.** What are the prospects for maintaining adequate consent? During a conflict, parties often try to control the delivery of humanitarian aid. They want to take credit for deliveries to their supporters and to prevent aid from reaching their adversaries. As a general rule, they are most likely to withdraw their consent when they believe that aid might erode their authority or diminish their hopes of victory. How are the parties likely to perceive that the humanitarian aid will affect their interests? Under what conditions might they want to deny aid to others or seize it for themselves? Will aid contribute to the causes of conflict?

During the Rwanda crisis of 1994, it was difficult to distribute humanitarian aid without contributing to the causes of conflict. The Hutu regular army and militia had committed genocide against the Tutsi minority in Rwanda, then fled when a Tutsi resistance movement seized power. Hutu officials initially controlled distribution of humanitarian aid among refugees in Zaire. As a result, that aid helped to maintain the authority of leaders responsible for genocide. Moreover, hoping to return by force, these leaders discouraged Hutu refugees from returning individually to Rwanda, now under a Tutsi-dominated government.

**Response to Withdrawal of Consent.** What response should be planned if one or more parties withdraw consent? The Security Council might respond with more-forceful measures, try to circumvent opposition from the parties, or terminate the operation. It might also consider incentives to increase consent. Is there sufficient international support for a forceful response? What incentives might entice the parties into allowing the distribution of aid? What would be the consequences if the peace force were to withdraw?

In Somalia during early 1993, the United States secured consent by deploying UNITAF, a highly capable task force. Confronted with this superior force, the faction leaders refrained from large-scale attacks, such as those occurring one month after UNITAF passed responsibility to the far-less-capable UNOSOM II. In Bosnia-Herzegovina, the United States and several European allies circumvented Bosnian Serb opposition on the ground by airdropping supplies into Muslim-held enclaves. In addition, UNPROFOR and the United Nations High Commissioner for Refugees sought to maintain consent from the

Bosnian Croats and Serbs by distributing humanitarian aid to all parties, regardless of need.

## Peace Enforcement

*Peace enforcement* is an attempt to coerce recalcitrant parties into complying with their agreements or with resolutions of the Security Council.

**Required Consent.** How much consent is required from the parties? Peace enforcement does not require consent; it begins when consent breaks down and the Security Council decides to coerce recalcitrant parties.[12] The Council states what it expects from the parties, and their compliance will restore consent to the peace operation. For example, in Bosnia-Herzegovina during 1994, the Security Council demanded that the parties comply with provisions concerning "safe areas,"[13] including weapons exclusion zones.

Continuing consent from some parties may be a prerequisite to success. In Somalia (1993) and Bosnia-Herzegovina (1993–1995), the Security Council attempted to coerce just one recalcitrant party (Aideed faction and Bosnian Serbs,[14] respectively), yet failed. The Council might well have hesitated to attempt peace enforcement against more than one party simultaneously.

---

[12]Up to the current time, every peace operation has begun with initial consent from the parties. But the Council is free to initiate peace enforcement without initial consent, and might even do so in some future case. In other words, the Council might decide to intervene impartially, holding all parties responsible and offering to coerce any party that defied the Council, without having obtained initial consent—perhaps even forcing entry into the region.

[13]Security Council Resolution 819 on April 16, 1993, declared the first "safe area" in Srebrenica: "Demands that all parties and others concerned treat Srebrenica and its surroundings as a safe area which should be free from any armed attack or any other hostile act." Security Council Resolution 824 on May 6, 1993, declared "safe areas" in Bihac, Gorazde, Sarajevo, Tuzla, and Zepa, using identical language. In both resolutions, the Security Council invoked Chapter VII.

[14]Both Bosnian Serbs and Muslims were supposed to comply with safe areas; consequently, peace enforcement might have affected either belligerent. But all six safe areas were Muslim-held and largely Muslim-inhabited, so the Security Council assumed it would have to proceed only against Serbs. Indeed, the ineffectual peace force ultimately withdrew entirely into Muslim-held territory to avoid being taken hostage by Bosnian Serb forces.

**Current Consent.** What actions by the parties would demonstrate that they have withdrawn their consent to the peace operation?

It may be difficult to discern when parties no longer consent to a peace operation, but the Security Council must make some determination or lose credibility. Declarations of intent are an unreliable indication. Indeed, even the most recalcitrant parties may repeatedly declare their adherence to the peace process as they interpret it.

Actions by the parties are a more certain indication. A party may be presumed to have withdrawn its consent when it flouts provisions of the peace process, defies resolutions of the Security Council, and opposes the peace force. *Opposition* might include restricting freedom of movement, harassing personnel, taking personnel hostage, and deliberately opening fire on the peace force.

On June 5, 1993, forces loyal to the United Somali Congress led by Mohammed Farah Aideed killed and mutilated Pakistani troops, leaving no doubt that this faction had withdrawn its consent. In 1993 and 1994, the Bosnian Serbs demonstrated their recalcitrance by refusing to carry out the Sarajevo airport agreements, obstructing the delivery of humanitarian aid, persistently bombarding safe areas, and repeatedly taking UNPROFOR personnel hostage under fire. When the Security Council attempted to enforce its will by authorizing NATO air attacks on the Bosnian Serbs, the Bosnian Serbs responded in April 1994 (Gorazde crisis), in November 1994 (Bihac crisis), and in May 1995 (Sarajevo crisis) by taking hundreds of UNPROFOR personnel hostage. These actions left no doubt that the Bosnian Serbs did not consent to safe areas or to the related exclusion zones.

**Prospects for Consent.** What are the prospects for restoring consent? Acquiescence of the recalcitrant parties would permit resumption of operations with consent. Those parties would be likely to acquiesce if they believed that the Security Council had the will and the means to enforce its resolutions and that these resolutions would be at least compatible with their aims.

In three cases of peace enforcement (Congo 1961–1962, Somalia 1993, Bosnia 1993–1995), the Security Council was disunited or displayed little determination. The peace forces were either marginally adequate or clearly inadequate to undertake peace enforcement successfully.[15] Recalcitrant parties were therefore encouraged to believe that they could defy the Security Council with impunity.

The first instance of peace enforcement was a protracted and ultimately successful effort by the United Nations Operation in the Congo (ONUC) to end the secession of Katanga Province, which was led by Moïse Tschombé with support from Belgian mining interests. In September 1961, Conor Cruise O'Brien, the chief U.N. official in Katanga, made an unsuccessful attempt (Operation *Morthor*) to defeat Tschombé's gendarmerie. U.N. Secretary-General Dag Hammarskjöld decided to negotiate with Tschombé, but he died in a plane crash while approaching Ndola airfield on the Congolese-Rhodesian border.

Western governments, especially France, were highly critical of operations against Katanga, causing the Security Council to act hesitantly. Finally, in December 1962, Major General Prem Chand, commanding an Indian brigade, seized Katanga (Operation Grandslam) and disarmed its gendarmerie and mercenaries, encountering very light resistance. The ostensible rationale was to restore ONUC's freedom of movement.

**Response to Withdrawal of Consent.** What responses should be planned if one or more parties withdraw consent? When a great power intervenes unilaterally in uncertain circumstances, its military staff routinely plans contingency operations. The Security Council has no military staff adequate for accomplishing such planning. In addition, the Council often works under political constraints that would inhibit contingency planning, even if an appropriate staff were available.

In several cases, initial consent was so fragile that it would have been prudent to plan responses to a breakdown. For example, when UNOSOM II assumed responsibility during May 1993, there was widespread doubt that the faction leaders would cooperate.

---

[15]In September 1995, a NATO bombing campaign led the Bosnian Serbs to restore the exclusion zone around Sarajevo and eventually to lift the siege. But successful Croatian Army offensives in Krajina and Bosnia-Herzegovina probably had more influence on the Serb decision than did the bombing campaign. The peace force on the ground in Bosnia-Herzegovina remained inadequate until after NATO assumed full control in December.

Mohammed Farah Aideed had a well-established reputation for ruthless ambition, which made his consent questionable, unless he faced a superior force. Secretary-General Boutros-Ghali expressed misgivings because U.S. forces had accomplished only limited disarmament before terminating UNITAF. Several NGOs expressed trepidation that UNOSOM II might not be able to provide sufficient security for their operations.

Despite these warnings, neither the Security Council nor the United States planned or prepared adequately for a withdrawal of consent. Following Aideed's attack on UNOSOM II during June, U.S. special-operations forces, supported by a battalion of U.S. mountain troops in light vehicles, attempted to capture the leadership of the United Somali Congress. U.S. special-operations forces conducted repeated heliborne assaults in Mogadishu until October 3, 1993, when several helicopters were downed and 18 Americans were killed. Unable to justify these losses, the Clinton Administration decided to withdraw U.S. forces from Somalia, leaving UNOSOM II ineffectual.

In retrospect, the United States should have planned to respond with much larger and more-capable forces to ensure a reasonable prospect of success without risking excessive casualties.

# Chapter Five

# MANDATE

Are the purpose and scope of the operation well defined?  Mandates define what is expected from the parties and what the peace force is expected to accomplish—in other words, its mission.  Of all the critical issues, those concerning mandates are the most easily resolved by the Security Council, because all mandates are ultimately based on its authority.  When time permits, the Security Council often requests the Secretary-General to investigate a conflict and recommend options.  The Council may then select among the options to frame a mandate.  When a member state offers to lead an operation and provide all or most of the forces—for example, the United States in Haiti and the French in Rwanda—that member state naturally has great influence on the mandate.

Every mandate should be sufficiently clear that the Force Commander understands what he is expected to accomplish.  But clarity alone is no guarantee of success.  A more fundamental issue is *feasibility:*  Can the peace force reasonably be expected to accomplish the tasks contained in the mandate?  Some tasks may yield to a more capable peace force than was originally planned.  Others, especially some associated with transition operations, may be inherently so difficult that even a very capable peace force will be frustrated.

Mandates also imply rules of engagement that should be appropriate to the situation and to the capabilities of the force.  Critics of peace operations often claim that the rules of engagement are too restrictive.  In fact, the rules have usually allowed harder measures than Force Commanders dared to take, in view of their forces' vulnerability. Finally, the Security Council needs to consider conditions for terminating an operation. If the Council decides to terminate when the mandate is accomplished, it can be trapped into an interminable operation, waiting for the parties to fulfill their parts. To avoid this trap, the Council may simply set a deadline, putting the parties on notice that they have only a limited time to make use of the opportunities afforded by the peace operation.

## PEACE-KEEPING

### Observation

**Clarity.** Are the provisions of the mandate clearly stated? Do the parties understand what is expected of them? *Clarity* implies that progress can be measured or evaluated in some reasonably straightforward way. For example, fewer reported incidents of fighting would indicate that parties are observing a cease-fire.

An observation mandate normally entails helping parties to implement their agreements. Agreements typically include cease-fire, disengagement, withdrawal of forces, and limitations on military activity. However, observation may include any provisions the parties wish to have verified by impartial observers. For example, the United Nations Observer Mission in El Salvador (ONUSAL) received a mandate to monitor a wide variety of agreements concluded between the government of El Salvador and the *Frente Farabundo Martí para la Liberación Nacional* (FMLN), including provisions respecting election procedures, judicial reform, and respect for human rights.

**Feasibility.** Can the observers reasonably be expected to conduct the tasks contained in the mandate?

In some cases, the Security Council has set unattainable objectives for observers. For example, the United Nations Observation Group in Lebanon (UNOGIL) was directed to ensure that there was no illegal infiltration of personnel or supply of arms or other materiel across the rugged Lebanese-Syrian border during a Lebanese civil war. This objective was unattainable, especially since Lebanese authorities could not provide security and since Syrian authorities refused to help.

**Rules of Engagement.** Are the rules of engagement appropriate? Do the rules of engagement reflect the circumstances of deployment and intent of the Security Council? Do they adequately provide for security of the observers?

When the intent is simply to help implement agreements, observers are usually unarmed and depend on the parties for security. But when observation is conducted in the context of more-demanding operations, military observers may have to defend themselves. For example, military observers in the context of a peace enforcement operation in Bosnia-Herzegovina returned fire to defend their observation posts. When observation is undertaken to deter violations, aggressive action is presumed likely; therefore, observers should either be armed for self-defense or prepared to evacuate.

**Termination.** Are conditions set for terminating the operation? If not, is an open-ended operation acceptable? Even a carefully prepared and fully agreed-upon peace plan offers no assurance that an operation will proceed on schedule. What delays would be acceptable? What behavior by the parties should be grounds for termination?

Termination is appropriate when the parties have implemented their agreements or when it becomes obvious that they will not implement their agreements, making the mandate unworkable. For example, operations were terminated in Lebanon (1958), Yemen (1964), and Afghanistan (1990) because the mandates became unworkable. In contrast, the United Nations Observer Group in Central America (ONUCA) and the First United Nations Angola Verification Mission (UNAVEM I) were terminated when they had successfully accomplished their mandates.

## Interposition

**Clarity.** Are the provisions of the mandate clearly stated? Does the mandate either delineate the buffer zone or provide a mechanism to define it? Does it state the peace force's responsibilities in controlling the buffer zone? Does it state the responsibilities of the parties with respect to each other and with respect to the interposition force? Does it include arrangements to resolve incidents and disputes?

A buffer zone is often based on the line of confrontation that has emerged between opposing forces during a conflict. Such a line may be poorly defined and hotly disputed. For example, delineation of the line of confrontation and, hence, the surrounding buffer zone, was highly contentious in Cyprus during 1974.

Interposition would be easier if the buffer zone were precisely defined before the peace force deployed, but risk of renewed hostility may compel an earlier start. For example, UNEF II was deployed while Egyptian and Israeli forces were still engaged, and there were constant violations of the cease-fire. Meeting at Kilometer 101 on the Cairo-Suez Highway on November 11, 1973, the Force Commander, Maj. Gen. Ensio P. H. Siilasvuo of Finland, and military representatives of Egypt and Israel signed an agreement to return to the positions occupied on October 22. Through this and subsequent agreements, the buffer zone and related provisions were eventually defined.[1]

**Feasibility.** Can the proposed peace force successfully interpose itself? The feasibility of an interposition mandate depends on the capabilities of the peace force, the terrain, and the character of the conflict. Interposition tends to be feasible between conventional forces with a zone delineated by terrain features. For example, the Suez Canal and the Gulf of Suez helped to delineate the buffer zone controlled by UNEF II after Israeli and Egyptian forces had disengaged. These parties deployed heavily armed forces in conventional fashion under firm control.

Interposition tends not to be feasible when the line of confrontation is tortuous or the parties operate in an unconventional fashion. For example, it would have been impracticable to delineate buffer zones between the opposing factions in Afghanistan during UNGOMAP, because the factions operated as light infantry, using raiding and infiltration tactics. For similar reasons, interposition would have been impracticable during the protracted civil war in Lebanon.

---

[1]After November 11, neither party withdrew its forces to the October 22 position as agreed. U.S. Secretary of State Henry Kissinger continued to conduct shuttle diplomacy, visiting Egypt and Israel in turn to mediate understandings and agreements that eventually ended the war and formed the basis for the UNEF II mandate.

**Rules of Engagement.**  Are the rules of engagement appropriate? Do the rules of engagement clearly distinguish conditions for employment of lethal force? Are they appropriate to the situations that the force is likely to be confronted by? In all cases, the rules of engagement have required that the peace force act with restraint and impartiality. The peace force has not usually been expected to defend the buffer zone, merely to control it. Lethal force has normally been authorized only in self-defense while accomplishing the mandate: At a minimum, peace forces are normally authorized to resist being forceably disarmed and abducted. They may also be authorized to protect their equipment and installations.

Depending on the situation, the force may have to confront political demonstrations, terrorism, raids by irregular forces, or incursions by conventional forces. For example, during July 1974, elements of the United Nations Peace-Keeping Force in Cyprus at the Nicosia Airport were confronted by Turkish forces. In this instance, the Turkish government agreed to respect the peace force, with the result that Nicosia Airport remains under UNFICYP control to this day. An interposition force may also have to provide services to civilian populations who reside in the buffer zone or who regularly transit the zone, as currently in Cyprus[2] and on the Golan Heights.

**Termination.**  Are conditions set for terminating the operation? If not, is an open-ended operation acceptable? What conditions would indicate that interposition could be terminated without incurring unacceptable risk of renewed conflict? If these conditions cannot be met, would the great powers be willing to support an open-ended operation?

Interposition has usually succeeded—sometimes at the price of becoming interminable. It can become a substitute for resolving conflict when parties have irreconcilable aims. Parties may prefer to perpetuate a buffer zone rather than to accept a political resolution they find unpalatable. They may also feel that interposition, even by a militarily insignificant force, increases their security by its implication that the Security Council will react to a large-scale incursion. Moreover, the great powers that initially supported an interposition

---

[2]The buffer zone in Cyprus encompasses 3 percent of the island. It includes several villages and some of the richest agricultural land.

mandate may prefer to perpetuate the operation rather than accept the risks of termination, especially if the operation can be made inexpensive. For these reasons, the Security Council has interposed forces in Cyprus and the Golan Heights for over two decades. In addition, a multilateral force continues to monitor activity in the Sinai, although not under United Nations auspices, because the Soviet Union declined to renew the U.N. mandate.

Even political settlement may not ensure termination of an interposition mandate. For example, the Golan Heights is strategic terrain that would enable Syria to oversee Galilee or Israel to threaten Damascus. If the Heights were entirely unoccupied, each party might fear that the other would seize the Heights in a sudden, rapid operation, gaining a significant military advantage. Therefore, the complete demilitarization of the Heights might create a less stable situation than if a force comparable to the current United Nations Disengagement Observer Force remained deployed, even following a comprehensive political agreement.

## MORE-AMBITIOUS OPERATIONS

### Transition

**Clarity.** Are the provisions of the mandate stated clearly? Does the mandate indicate the tasks that military and civilian components are expected to accomplish? Does it spell out the responsibilities of the parties? Is there mutual understanding concerning the parties' various responsibilities?

Transition usually includes a variety of interrelated tasks to be performed by military and civilian components of the mission and by the parties. In addition, the contributions of non-governmental organizations may be vital. What is expected from the parties and from the military and civilian components of the mission should be explicitly stated and mutually understood.

For example, during the Cambodia operation, several provisions of the mandate caused contention. According to the PDK (Khmer Rouge) interpretation of the Paris Agreement, UNTAC should have replaced the existing government with a coalition of the four factions, not merely monitored the existing government's activities, prior to the national elections. The provision to oversee withdrawal of "foreign forces" also caused contention. All of the Cambodian factions, but especially the PDK, used a broad definition of *foreign forces*, tending to include all persons of Vietnamese origin. Had UNTAC accepted such a broad definition, it would have abetted the forcible removal of non-Khmer to satisfy the Cambodian dislike of foreigners. In practice, UNTAC refused to proceed against settlers of Vietnamese origin, even if they were former members of the Vietnamese army and still possessed weapons, as many did in a country that was awash in weapons.

**Feasibility.** Can the provisions of the mandate be accomplished, considering especially the capabilities of the peace force, likely cooperation from the parties, and the society and culture of the people? Assessment of feasibility may entail understanding not just the political-military situation but also the society and culture of the peoples involved, especially their support for democratic practice.

For example, the Cambodia operation might have failed entirely had the Cambodian people not enthusiastically supported an election. In March 1992, when UNTAC began operations in Cambodia, the government was corrupt and inefficient; the factions were hostile and suspicious of each other; armed marauders plagued the civilian population; and the countryside was thickly strewn with land mines.[3] Under such circumstances and given its limited capabilities, UNTAC had to abandon disarmament, arguably the heart of its mandate. But the Cambodian people, weary of protracted civil war and occupation, enthusiastically supported national elections, which became the most notable accomplishment of UNTAC.

The United Nation Mission in Haiti (UNMIH) may also owe its greatest success to popular support for democracy. In June 1995, UNMIH, including elements of the U.S. 25th Infantry Division (Light) and Special Forces, provided security for national elections in Haiti. Because of prevailing illiteracy, most Haitians used party symbols to

---

[3]Cambodia was plagued by thousands of mines laid by all factions over decades. During its first year of operations, UNTAC supervised clearance of 15,000 mines but estimated that the Cambodians would need 20 years or more to eliminate the problem, assuming that no more mines were laid. UNTAC officials believed that the PDK was continuing to lay mines during the peace operation.

identify their candidates. However, all but one of the major parties supported the highly popular President Jean-Bertrand Aristide, leaving the voters little choice. Still, it was a major accomplishment to hold free elections in a country that had historically suffered from dictatorship and brutal repression.

It remains to be seen whether Cambodians and Haitians will seize their opportunities or fall back into the civil strife and oppressive regimes that have blighted their pasts. Their prospects depend far more on their own societies and cultures than on any outside influences.

**Rules of Engagement.** In authorizing a transition operation, the Security Council might invoke Chapter VI, implying self-defense of the peace force, or it might invoke Chapter VII, implying willingness to coerce parties through combat operations if necessary. If Chapter VI is invoked, do the rules of engagement allow the peace force to protect itself adequately? If Chapter VII is invoked, do the rules of engagement accord the Force Commander enough freedom of action to accomplish his mandate?

In Cambodia, UNTAC operated under Chapter VI, which implies that it would use force in self-defense while accomplishing its mandate. The peace force consisted of infantry without supporting arms and was greatly outnumbered by the armed factions. Invocation of Chapter VI accorded with the policies of the participating countries, whose governments were willing to assist the Cambodian peace process but were unwilling to conduct a military campaign. Under these circumstances, the Force Commander, Lt. Gen. John M. Sanderson of Australia, thought that more-liberal rules of engagement, especially when applied to the PDK (Khmer Rouge), would have provoked dangerous retaliation.[4]

In Bosnia-Herzegovina, the Security Council authorized a transition operation under Chapter VII and eventually attempted peace enforcement, especially to maintain safe areas. Despite this ambitious

---

[4]Sanderson's deputy, Maj. Gen. Michel Loridon of France, strongly disagreed, asserting that UNTAC could defeat the PDK at the cost of several hundred casualties. Loridon considered such casualties an acceptable cost for solving the Khmer Rouge problem. This disagreement was resolved by Loridon's reassignment.

mandate, UNPROFOR rules of engagement stayed restrictive: As a general rule, elements of UNPROFOR were not allowed to return fire or to receive close air support unless actually engaged.[5] But the real problem was limited capability, not restrictive rules of engagement. Indeed, the rules of engagement would have permitted more-resolute action than Force Commanders considered prudent for their weak and scattered forces.

**Termination.** Are conditions set for terminating the operation? If not, is an open-ended operation acceptable? Should the operation be kept to a schedule or be keyed to cooperation, in effect becoming open-ended? If open-ended, what conditions would demonstrate that the mandate had been accomplished? What conditions would indicate that the mandate should be changed or abandoned? An interminable transition would be a contradiction in terms and probably an unacceptable expense. But in several cases, the Security Council has keyed an operation to cooperation from the parties, thus making the operation open-ended.

Cyprus and Croatia provide examples of open-ended transition operations. In Cyprus, Secretary-General U Thant initially assumed that UNFICYP would assist Greek Cypriots and Turkish Cypriots in returning to normal conditions, presuming their cooperation in some kind of central government. But when the Turkish Cypriots refused to accept minority status in any government, the Security Council accepted an open-ended operation. For roughly a decade (1964–1974), UNFICYP attempted unsuccessfully to induce the two opposing communities to cooperate with each other.

In Croatia, the Security Council established UNPROFOR in March 1992 as an interim arrangement to create the conditions of peace and security required for negotiating an overall settlement of the

---

[5]When an element of UNPROFOR was taken under fire and requested close air support, the engagement had to continue long enough for the aircraft to arrive over target and to deliver ordnance. If, as happened on several occasions, the hostile party broke off engagement in the meantime, the request for close air support was negated. A hostile party can exploit such restrictive rules of engagement to protect itself. Whenever it is getting the worst of an exchange or fears the arrival of greater firepower, it can escape harm by breaking contact.

Yugoslav crisis.[6]  Such a settlement depended on the willingness of Serbia, Croatia, and Krajina (the Croatian Serb authority in Knin) to reach agreement, which was not forthcoming. So the operation became open-ended, marking time until Croatia regained Krajina by force in August 1995.

In the more usual pattern, the Security Council sets a schedule for the transition operation.  In Cambodia, for example, a time frame was set for achieving objectives in each phase of the peace plan. Despite a slow start, UNTAC stayed almost on schedule.  When the PDK refused to disarm during Phase Two, UNTAC simply continued on to the election activities planned for Phase Three, taking a risk that the PDK would not disrupt the elections.

## Security for Humanitarian Aid

**Clarity.**  Are the provisions of the mandate clearly stated?  Does the mandate set forth what cooperation is expected from the parties and what the peace force is expected to accomplish?  Are limits set to prevent expansion of the mandate?  Conversely, what expansion would be acceptable?  The parties should understand how much freedom of action they must accord to the peace force.  The Force Commander needs to understand what degree of protection he must provide and the scope of humanitarian aid.  It is difficult to distinguish between security for aid and security for the population that receives that aid.[7]  Providing security for aid shades almost imperceptibly into establishing more-generalized conditions of security. As a result, this type of operation has a natural tendency to expand.

Somalia illustrates inherent pressure to expand humanitarian aid operations.  When the warring factions continually obstructed deliv-

---

[6]In March 1992, only Yugoslavia (Serbia and Montenegro) and Croatia were engaged in active hostilities.  A month later, the Yugoslav crisis expanded to include even more-complex and more-intractable fighting in Bosnia-Herzegovina.  The Croatian Serbs in Krajina were closely associated with the Bosnian Serbs, making it difficult to resolve either conflict in isolation.

[7]For example, on some occasions during the Somalia operation, U.S. forces discovered that bandits were robbing people of humanitarian aid after the recipients had left the points where it was distributed.  To be certain that aid was consumed by the intended recipients, U.S. forces would have been compelled to secure entire communities, not just the distribution points.

ery of aid, President George Bush ordered an operation to secure its delivery. The Bush Administration and the following Clinton Administration explicitly defined the mandate as security for humanitarian aid, excluding more-ambitious efforts at disarmament.

The U.S. Commander in Chief, Central Command (USCINCCENT), clearly articulated this mission and strenuously resisted expanding it. But exigencies on the scene ultimately led to performing considerable disarmament.[8] UNITAF disarmed individuals carrying unauthorized weapons and also supported implementation of the agreements concluded by the parties on January 8 and 15 in Addis Ababa. As a practical matter, the most effective way to secure humanitarian aid was to disarm the uncontrolled bandits and, more important, the political militias, as agreed in Addis Ababa.

**Feasibility.**    Given its capabilities and the expected level of cooperation from parties, can the peace force be expected to secure humanitarian aid adequately?

In Somalia, conditions were so unsettled and the factions, especially in the port cities of Mogadishu and Kismayu, so violently opposed to each other, that security could be ensured only if the participating states could quickly deploy large and highly capable forces. As a practical matter, the mandate would become feasible only if the United States were willing to act as lead state. No other state was willing to provide the required combat forces and logistics support.

In operations in Bosnia-Herzegovina, UNPROFOR had, among other things, the task of securing humanitarian aid. Opposition came from Bosnian Serbs who were besieging Muslim-held enclaves. Although operating under Chapter VII, UNPROFOR was too weak to compel passage of convoys, so allowed the Bosnian Serbs to obstruct them for months at a time. In Sarajevo, UNPROFOR usually managed to keep the airport open for relief flights while acquiescing to Bosnian

---

[8]Subsequently, there was much discussion about "mission creep" in Somalia. UNITAF experienced "mission creep": It was told to secure humanitarian aid and actually did much more. But this mission creep did not endanger UNITAF or greatly delay its departure. UNOSOM II (supported by U.S. forces) did *not* experience mission creep: It began life with an ambitious mandate to implement disarmament and was soon directed to enforce peace against General Aideed. These decisions concerning UNOSOM II were deliberate and cannot be characterized as "creep."

Serb control over land routes into the city. This part of the UNPROFOR mandate was not feasible unless UNPROFOR was heavily reinforced or the Muslim side opened land routes to the enclaves.

**Rules of Engagement.** Are the rules of engagement appropriate? Security operations imply that the Security Council is willing to employ force beyond strict self-defense of the peace force and so, ideally, should invoke Chapter VII. In some circumstances, security operations may require very liberal rules of engagement. Do the rules of engagement allow the force to protect itself adequately and to secure the facilities and activities associated with humanitarian aid? Do they provide for adequate flexibility to cope with unforeseen difficulties?

In Somalia, UNITAF operated under Chapter VII, with rules of engagement promulgated by the U.S. Central Command (USCENTCOM). Once the Security Council had approved the Addis Ababa accords, UNITAF was authorized to use all necessary force to disarm groups or individuals in areas under its control.[9] A contentious issue concerned security guards employed by NGOs, often at extremely high rates. NGOs complained that their guards had been disarmed by UNITAF, especially when crossing sector boundaries. To solve this problem, UNITAF planned to initiate a country-wide system of weapon permits.

Given the lawless conditions in Somalia, UNITAF clearly needed liberal rules of engagement to be effective. It was authorized to use lethal force to counter hostile action or hostile intent, and it was allowed to forcefully disarm groups or individuals in areas under its control. UNITAF seized heavy weapons and "technicals" (light vehicles mounting crew-served weapons), destroyed caches of weapons and ammunition, and prevented Somalis from displaying weapons unless authorized to do so. Somalis quickly learned that U.S. soldiers would not open fire on children, even if they threw

---

[9]The following classes of weapons were subject to immediate confiscation: all weapons not under direct control of a person; all weapons displayed in any manner that demonstrated hostile intent; all machine guns, recoilless rifles, mortars, rocket-propelled grenade (RPG) launchers, and all crew-served weapons; all "technicals" (light vehicles mounting crew-served weapons); and all armored vehicles.

rocks and attempted to steal valuable items. U.S. troops were plagued by such incidents until they developed nonlethal counter-measures, which included using tent pegs, batons, and cayenne pepper spray. The spray was so effective that, by the end of the operation, U.S. soldiers could disperse Somalis simply by waving any aerosol can.[10]

**Termination.** Are conditions set for terminating the operation? If not, is an open-ended operation acceptable? Alleviation of suffering might be a condition to terminate the operation. But if conflict continued, suffering might ensue again, possibly prompting deeper involvement. Can humanitarian aid be secured without deeper involvement in the conflict? If deeper involvement is acceptable, what type of operation would be most appropriate?

In Somalia, a security operation under UNITAF was followed by a transition operation under UNOSOM II, which was intended to address the causes of conflict by facilitating the reconciliation of the warring factions in a new national government. In this case, a successful security operation was the precursor to an unsuccessful attempt at transition.

UNAMIR also illustrates the difficulty of terminating a security operation. Following the French Operation Turquoise, UNAMIR was mandated to secure continued delivery of humanitarian aid, with a possible role in national reconciliation. By early 1995, UNAMIR was no longer welcomed by the Tutsi-dominated Rwandan Patriotic Front (RPF), which wanted to dissolve the refugee camps in Rwanda. At the same time, refugee camps in neighboring Zaire were becoming bases for Hutu militias that might attempt to invade Rwanda from Zaire as the RPF had done from Uganda. Understandably, few member states were willing to contribute forces to operations in Rwanda, yet the Security Council hesitated to terminate operations for fear of precipitating a new round of fighting.

---

[10]Jonathan T. Dworken, "Rules of Engagement: Lessons from Restore Hope," *Military Review*, September 1994, p. 30.

## Peace Enforcement

**Clarity.** Are the provisions of the mandate stated clearly?  Since peace enforcement implies combat operations, the mandate should specify or infer what military objectives the Force Commander is expected to accomplish.  The mandate should also inform the parties about how they are expected to comply.  Does the mandate specify or imply what military objectives the Force Commander is expected to accomplish?  Are these objectives sufficiently clear that a Force Commander can estimate what forces he will need, can accomplish operational planning, and can conduct appropriate combat operations?  Are the parties clearly informed of the compliance expected of them?

Clarity is no guarantee of success.  The Security Council gave UNOSOM II a clear transition mandate and subsequently announced a clear change to peace enforcement.  On March 26, 1993, the Security Council passed Resolution 814 invoking Chapter VII and mandating UNOSOM II to assist in humanitarian relief, to promote political reconciliation under the Addis Ababa agreements, and to establish a Somali national police force.  On June 6, 1993, after Aideed's followers attacked UNOSOM II, the Security Council passed Resolution 837 reaffirming that the Secretary-General was authorized to take "all necessary measures" under Chapter VII against those responsible for armed attacks and urging member states to provide tanks, personnel carriers, and attack helicopters so that UNOSOM II could confront and deter armed attacks.  The Security Council has never issued a clearer mandate for peace enforcement than it did in Somalia, yet the operation ended in nearly complete failure.[11]

**Feasibility.** Are the provisions of the mandate feasible?  Is the mandate feasible given the capabilities of the peace force and the resistance that recalcitrant parties are likely to offer?  To what extent is the

---

[11]While clarity helps, size and capabilities of the peace force have been more important.  In the Congo, the mandate was vague and ambiguous, but the Indian brigade was strong enough to at least end the Katangan secession.  In Somalia (UNOSOM II) and Bosnia-Herzegovina (UNPROFOR–NATO), the mandates were much clearer, but weakness led to catastrophic failures.

peace force vulnerable to retaliation?  What participation of outside powers is required?

When the Security Council decided to apprehend General Aideed in Somalia, the mandate remained feasible only so long as the United States was willing to lead.  It immediately ceased to be feasible when the United States backed down after suffering casualties in a special operation.  The complete withdrawal of U.S. forces occasioned the withdrawal of European forces and left UNOSOM II with an unworkable mandate, unless the warring factions had unexpectedly compromised on their differences.

As regards Bosnia-Herzegovina, the Security Council continually expanded the mandate, often adding provisions that were not feasible. Generally speaking, provisions that could be enforced by NATO in the airspace above Bosnia-Herzegovina and in the Adriatic Sea were feasible; those that required UNPROFOR to act on the ground were not feasible.

During late 1994, UNPROFOR became hostage to the Bosnian Serbs, preventing NATO from making full use of its air power.  NATO initially enforced a no-fly zone for fixed-wing aircraft over Bosnia-Herzegovina, allowing helicopters to fly.  But by early 1995, UNPROFOR's weakness was limiting NATO's ability to enforce even this provision.[12]  NATO began to regain freedom of action after UNPROFOR redeployed its forces to reduce its exposure to hostage-taking.

NATO sea power enforced an arms embargo in the Adriatic, even after the United States refused unilaterally to participate.  Provisions of the mandate concerning security for humanitarian aid were not fea-

---

[12]Bosnian Serbs fired on NATO aircraft many times, but, with few exceptions, missed their targets.  In April 1994, the Serbs shot down a British Harrier while the pilot was trying to attack Serb armor near Gorazde.  In late 1994, the Bosnian Serbs began to establish an air defense system that included medium- and long-range surface-to-air missiles (SA-2, SA-6).  NATO officials requested permission to suppress these missiles after NATO aircraft were illuminated by the associated radars, but UNPROFOR refused permission because it feared retaliation against UNPROFOR.  In June 1995, the Serbs employed an SA-6 to shoot down a U.S. F-16 flying a routine counter-air mission (Operation Deny Flight).  At the same time, the SRSG refused permission to attack a Serb airfield at Banja Luka that supported sorties of ground attack aircraft, again from fear of retaliation against UNPROFOR.

sible for land convoys, prompting NATO to airland and airdrop supplies.  In the end, provisions for protecting safe areas were not feasible, again because of weakness in ground forces.

**Rules of Engagement.**  Are the rules of engagement appropriate?  Is the change to peace enforcement adequately reflected in the rules of engagement?  Are the rules appropriate for situations facing the Force Commander?  Do they allow sufficient freedom of action to conduct effective combat operations?

In the Congo, ONUC was initially limited to self-defense under a fairly liberal interpretation.  For example, ONUC was authorized to open fire if other forces moved close to its positions or attempted to surround them.  Such permissive rules were necessary to prevent larger forces from overwhelming relatively small ONUC detachments.

ONUC was also authorized to use force to ensure its own freedom of movement.  In February 1961, the rules were expanded to allow use of force as a last resort to prevent civil war.  In November 1961, they were expanded again to allow use of force to apprehend mercenaries.  But the shift to offensive operations against Katanga was not acknowledged, because it was highly contentious within the Security Council.  When Katangan forces fired on ONUC, ONUC seized this pretext to execute Operation Grandslam, which culminated in disarming or dispersing the Katangan gendarmerie and mercenaries in Katangan service.  Ostensibly, this operation was conducted to secure freedom of movement for the force, but the actual purpose was to end the secession of Katanga Province.

In three cases of peace enforcement, the rules of engagement have not always been appropriate, but neither have they been a major cause of failure.  In the Congo, ONUC made do with vague rules that allowed considerable latitude.  In Somalia, U.S.–controlled forces and UNOSOM II were inhibited by rules designed to limit collateral damage in Mogadishu, but the causes of failure lay elsewhere.  In Bosnia-Herzegovina, fearing retaliation, UNPROFOR limited itself far more strictly than its rules of engagement required.[13]  Although

---

[13]UNPROFOR personnel might use their weapons to defend themselves, other U.N. personnel, and areas under their protection.  If taken hostage under fire, they were to

NATO was constantly ready to provide close air support, UNPROFOR almost never called for support, even when taken hostage under attack. With few exceptions, such as anti-sniping patrols in Sarajevo, UNPROFOR seldom employed force to protect the safe areas. The rules of engagement, which were quite liberal, were not the problem; UNPROFOR's weakness was.

**Termination.** Are conditions set for terminating the operation? If not, is an open-ended operation acceptable? What conditions would establish compliance and permit return to operations with consent? What conditions would indicate that peace enforcement had failed and should be abandoned? How should limits be set to avoid an interminable operation that becomes intolerable for the participants?

Lesser operations might become open-ended without undue risk or expense. But open-ended peace enforcement would become intolerable, both for the participating member states and for the U.N. as an organization.

The Security Council has often allowed peace enforcement to drag on for extended periods without achieving definite results. The Congo operation lasted four years and ended with the country still gripped by violence. The return of Katanga Province simply provided a convenient point for terminating an operation that was highly unpopular and disruptive to the U.N. The Somalia operation lasted almost three years and ended with Mogadishu still torn by conflict. After the United States announced its withdrawal, the peace force marked time until the United States secured its evacuation. The operation in Bosnia-Herzegovina lasted over three and one-half years under U.N. control,[14] despite repeated, and sometimes catastrophic,

---

take immediate protective measures and warn the aggressor of their intent to use force. If hostile action threatened their lives, they were to open fire, on orders of the local commander. They were authorized to resist military or paramilitary incursions into protected areas and safe areas. They were prohibited from taking actions that might cause collateral damage, i.e., damage to other than the intended targets. *Force Commander's Policy Directive 13*, UNPROFOR Headquarters, Zagreb, July 19, 1993.

[14]On March 13, 1992, Lt. Gen. Satish Nambiar of India established UNPROFOR headquarters in Sarajevo, although his forces were deployed in Croatia. This location had been chosen in the hope that UNPROFOR's presence would have a calming effect on the parties. On December 20, 1995, in a ceremony at Sarajevo airport, the NATO South Commander, Admiral Leighton W. Smith, formally assumed operational control over those UNPROFOR units that were incorporated into IFOR.

failures to accomplish key provisions of the mandate. That operation is still in progress, but under NATO control and with much greater success.

# Chapter Six

# CHARACTER OF THE PEACE FORCE

Is the peace force configured appropriately for its mandate? Like any military force, a peace force should be properly armed, equipped, and controlled to accomplish its mission, which is equivalent to its mandate in the context of peace operations. Appropriate configuration can vary from unarmed observers to a heavily armed combined task force.

Control over combat operations is a central issue for any peace force operating under Chapter VII. The U.N. system is not suitable to control combat operations, because member states have not fully implemented relevant articles of the Charter and are unlikely to do so. Therefore, when the Security Council invokes Chapter VII, it should select some agent, usually a lead state or regional alliance, that can control combat operations effectively. The Security Council often authorizes U.N.–controlled operations simultaneously or sequentially with operations controlled by its agents. In such cases, the operations should be properly related to each other. For example, the relationship between UNPROFOR and NATO in Bosnia-Herzegovina was contradictory and self-defeating.

Issues concerning the peace force include capabilities, size, composition, and control. The Secretary-General often has difficulty assembling a force with the required capabilities, especially transport, engineers, and medical units, unless great powers are enthusiastic participants. The force should be sized appropriately for its tasks and area of operations. Its composition by national contingent should ensure impartiality and efficiency. In recent years, the Council has departed significantly from its traditional practice of excluding contributors notoriously sympathetic to one side.  Had it not departed from this principle, France would have been excluded from Rwanda and the United States and Russia would have been excluded from Bosnia-Herzegovina.  In these examples, impartiality was maintained, but the new practice harbors a risk that peace forces might join in the conflict.  Apart from Chapter VII operations, control through the U.N. system is usually adequate, but barely so for the larger transition operations.

## CONTROL OVER COMBAT OPERATIONS[1]

The U.N. system is adequate to control peace-keeping and also more-ambitious operations that do not demand combat beyond self-defense.  It usually features a Force Commander responsible to a Special Representative of the Secretary-General, who is supported by a small multinational staff assembled ad hoc.  But the U.N. system is not adequate to control combat operations, because Articles 43, 45, 46, and 47 of the Charter have not been fully implemented.

Recognizing this lack, the Security Council has not attempted to control large-scale enforcement actions through the U.N.[2]  For peace enforcement, the Security Council has used several expedients, employing the U.N. system but also various agents:  lead states, regional

---

[1]Control over forces is distinct from command authority, which normally remains with sovereign states.  States do not relinquish command over their forces to other states unless *in extremis*.  To create a multilateral force, states grant operational or tactical control over their forces, i.e., temporary subordination to effect a common purpose.  For example, Britain and France granted operational control over their forces to the U.S. Commander in Chief, Central Command, during the recent Persian Gulf War.  As another example, the Supreme Allied Commander in Europe (SACEUR) controls no forces during peacetime in this capacity, but he is simultaneously Commander in Chief, United States European Command.  In this capacity, he commands U.S. forces deployed in Europe and designated for NATO.  During wartime, he would exercise operational control, not command, over forces contributed by member states to the alliance.  At this level, command authority is an attribute of sovereignty, expressing a state's ultimate responsibility and concern for its military forces.

[2]In two cases of enforcement, the Security Council either designated an executive agent (Korean War) or broadly authorized member states to act, allowing them to select agents (Persian Gulf War).  During the Korean War, the United States served as executive agent.  During the Persian Gulf War, two agents formed a coalition: USCINCCENT controlled Western forces; the Saudi Joint Force Commander controlled Islamic forces.

security organizations, and coalitions.[3]  It has combined U.N.–controlled operations with operations under control of other agents, both simultaneously and sequentially, as summarized in Figure 6.1.

The Security Council might authorize a single operation under the U.N. system, but at the price of inadequate control.  Inadequate control contributed to failure in the Congo, although the underlying cause was lack of consensus in the Security Council.  The Katangan secession was quashed by an Indian brigade acting under instructions from a home government that opposed the secession for ideological reasons.

Choice of the U.N. system also imposes limitations on the force: According to a long-established principle, no single participant is supposed to contribute more than one-third of the force.

RAND*MR583-6.1*

| | Description | Examples | Risks |
|---|---|---|---|
| Single Operation— U.N. Control | Security Council authorizes an operation through the U.N. system. | ONUC in the Congo | Inadequate control over combat operations |
| Single Operation— Authority Delegated | Security Council delegates its authority to an agent. | None | Divergence between Security Council and its agent |
| Operations in Sequence— Various Control Arrangements | An agent relinquishes control to U.N. | UNITAF to UNOSOM II in Somalia; MNF to UNMIH in Haiti | Failure to properly relate successive operations |
| | U.N. relinquishes control to an agent. | UNPROFOR to IFOR in Bosnia-Herzegovina | |
| Operations Simultaneously— Various Control Arrangements | An agent controls combat operations; U.N. controls less-demanding operations. | U.S. forces and UNOSOM II in Somalia; NATO and UNPROFOR in Bosnia-Herzegovina; ECOMOG and UNOMIL in Liberia | Divergence in strategy; retaliation against forces under U.N. control |

Figure 6.1—Options for Control of Forces

---

[3]"Any large scale participation of U.S. forces in a major peace enforcement operation that is likely to involve combat should ordinarily be conducted through U.S. command and operational control or through competent regional organizations such as NATO or ad hoc coalitions." U.S. Department of State, *Administration's Policy*, 1994, p. 2.

The Council might authorize a single operation under an agent, analogous to enforcement in Korea and Kuwait, but has not done so. For example, beginning in 1992, the Security Council welcomed efforts in Liberia by the Economic Community of West African States (ECOWAS) through an ECOWAS Monitoring Group (ECOMOG). ECOMOG, especially the dominant Nigerian contingent, undertook some peace enforcement actions. But in September 1993, the Council established a simultaneous operation, the United Nations Observer Mission in Liberia (UNOMIL), which was responsible to the Secretary-General. UNOMIL received a mandate requiring extensive coordination with ECOMOG.[4]

The Security Council might authorize sequential operations: a non–U.N. operation followed by a U.N.–controlled operation, or vice versa. For example, the Council authorized UNITAF, a U.S.–led coalition, to secure humanitarian aid in Somalia and to establish secure conditions for hand-over to UNOSOM II. Conversely, the Council directed UNPROFOR to release its units to IFOR, a combatant command within NATO charged with implementing the General Framework Agreement for Peace in Bosnia and Herzegovina (Dayton Agreements). There is risk that successive operations may not be properly related to each other, as is well exemplified by operations in Somalia.

Alternatively, the Security Council might authorize simultaneous operations: a U.N.–controlled operation coordinated with an operation controlled by another agent. Several risks are associated with this alternative. The agent and the U.N. Force Commander may have different perspectives, leading to divergent strategies that cannot easily be harmonized. This alternative may also expose the U.N.–controlled force to retaliation from parties suffering from actions conducted by the other agent. For example, during 1993–1995, the different perspectives of UNPROFOR and NATO led to divergent strategies that caused persistent disagreement and frustration.

---

[4]Security Council Resolution 866 on September 22, 1993, mandated UNOMIL to investigate violations of the cease-fire, monitor compliance with the arms embargo on Liberia, verify the election process, assist humanitarian activities, help ECOMOG to clear mines, and coordinate with ECOMOG in discharging ECOMOG's separate responsibilities without participating in enforcement.

Moreover, Bosnian Serbs retaliated for NATO air actions by attacking vulnerable UNPROFOR ground forces and taking them hostage.

## PEACE-KEEPING

Peace-keeping demands basic infantry units that are widely available, although quality varies greatly among member states. During initial deployment and any subsequent crises, quality may be a matter of special concern. In addition, peace-keeping often requires support, such as medical units, engineers, signals, and in-theater airlift. The U.N. has chronic difficulty finding member states that are able and willing to make such support available.

### Observation

**Capabilities.** Does the peace force have the required capabilities? Parties are more likely to honor agreements if they believe that impartial observers will detect any significant violations. They may lose confidence if they believe that other parties can violate agreements without being detected. Therefore, observers should be able to cover the area of interest, detect violations, and report promptly. Observers are also often expected to mediate and resolve violations, creating a need for skilled and experienced negotiators.

Do the observers have sufficient mobility to cover the area of interest? Do they have surveillance capabilities required to detect violations? Are communications adequate for operational control, interface with the parties, and links to higher headquarters? Are there personnel with the experience and negotiating skills needed to resolve reported violations? Is the required logistics support available? If the parties will not provide security, can the observers defend themselves or withdraw in a timely fashion?

The heavily bureaucratic U.N. procurement system has impeded operations through delays in providing logistics support. For example, the UNAVEM II initially deployed without proper housing, potable water, or sources of electrical power, even though U.N. authorities were well acquainted with Angola through UNAVEM I. On other occasions, lack of equipment has impeded operations. For example, the United Nations Yemen Observer Mission lacked sufficient aircraft to cover the rugged, ill-defined border between Saudi Arabia and Yemen. As a result, UNYOM could not confirm that either Egypt or Saudi Arabia was fulfilling its commitment to disengage from the civil war in Yemen.

**Size.** Is the force sufficiently large?

Accomplishing the mandate can depend on each party's belief that the peace force is large enough to maintain reliable, continuous coverage over areas where the other party might try to gain a military advantage. If the peace force is too small to maintain this coverage, it will lose credibility. For example, the small United Nations Observation Group in Lebanon repeatedly faced situations that demanded more manpower. Its inadequate size was largely due to the slow process of recruiting national contingents.[5]

**Composition.** Does the composition of the peace force by national contingents ensure impartiality? Can the participating member states provide the required capabilities?

The U.N. has often drawn experienced observers and skilled mediators from current operations, such as the United Nations Truce Supervision Organization, as well as soliciting member states for fresh contributions. During the Cold War, great powers were presumed to be partial, but the end of the Cold War removed this presumption.[6] For example, China, France, Russia, and the United States contribute military observers to the United Nations Mission for the Referendum in Western Sahara. But any member state, including great powers, might be considered unsuitable if it had a notorious bias.

**Control.** Is the peace force adequately controlled, especially considering possible combat? Observers are normally unarmed or lightly armed for self-defense, and therefore U.N. control is adequate. This

---

[5]UNOGIL began operations in June 1958 with only 94 observers to cover the entire border between Lebanon and Syria, plus the major Mediterranean seaports. By November, there were 500 ground observers and 90 air observers, but by that time UNOGIL was near termination. Mona Ghali, "United Nations Observation Group in Lebanon, 1958," in Durch, *The Evolution of UN Peacekeeping,* 1993, pp. 170–171.

[6]As an exception, France and the United States each contributed 21 military observers to UNTSO (then known as the Truce Commission) in Palestine during 1948.

control is usually exercised through a Chief Military Observer (CMO) appointed by the Secretary-General.

## Interposition

**Capabilities.** Does the force have the required capabilities? With the exception of IFOR, interposition forces have been configured to control buffer zones, but not to defend those zones against large-scale incursion. Can the peace force control the buffer zone by detecting and challenging violations? Can it detect violations of agreements to restrict military activities outside the buffer zone? Does it have sufficient mobility and protection to operate successfully in the expected environment?

Interposition forces are usually organized and equipped as light or mechanized infantry battalions, depending on the situation. They are normally expected to defend themselves while accomplishing the mandate. For example, the United Nations Peace-Keeping Force in Cyprus was lightly armed and equipped prior to the Turkish intervention in 1974. In response to this intervention, UNFICYP temporarily acquired heavier infantry weapons and armored vehicles.

**Size.** Is the force large enough to detect violations throughout the buffer zone? After detecting violations, is it large enough to challenge violators in a credible fashion?

Buffer zones have varied from the relatively compact Golan Heights[7] to the long, meandering line of confrontation between Croatian forces and Croatian Serb forces in Krajina. In the latter case, UNCRO and the civilian police component observed the line of confrontation from widely spaced observation posts and conducted roving patrols. Forces committed to interposition have ranged from 1,300 to 7,000 personnel, not including IFOR. To date, the largest such force has been UNEF II, with 7,000 personnel in 1974. But this strength was minuscule compared with that of the parties, Egypt alone having some 800,000 active-duty soldiers at the time.

---

[7]On the Golan Heights, the buffer zone generally follows the front line between Israeli and Syrian forces that existed in May 1974. It extends from Mount Hermon in the north to the Jordanian border in the south, a distance of roughly 80 km.

**Composition.** Does the composition of the peace force by national contingents ensure impartiality? Can the participating member states provide the required capabilities? Will the contributing member states provide qualified, well-disciplined personnel? Will there be personnel with sufficient experience in peace-keeping operations?

Many states can provide reasonably well-trained light or mechanized infantry battalions. But interposition can also require a judicious mixture of firmness and finesse, especially during an initial phase. Therefore, the Secretary-General has often solicited contributions from states with proven records in peace-keeping.

As an example, the United Nations Disengagement Observer Force on the Golan Heights included contingents from Austria, Canada, Finland, Iran, Peru, and Poland, and commanders were typically drawn from Austria, a highly experienced contributor. As another example, UNFICYP had contingents from Australia, Austria, Britain, Canada, Denmark, Finland, Ireland, New Zealand, and Sweden, and commanders were typically drawn from Austria, India, and British Commonwealth countries.

**Control.** Is the peace force adequately controlled, especially considering possible combat? Does the Force Commander have sufficient authority and adequate staff? Are there appropriate channels for resolving violations? If required, is the Force Commander prepared to act as an intermediary among the parties?

Interposition forces are usually not expected to engage in combat beyond self-defense; therefore, U.N. control is adequate.[8] They are typically controlled through a Force Commander responsible to the Special Representative of the Secretary-General or to the Secretary-General directly. Force Commanders are often selected from member states with experience in peace operations. They are supported by small combined staffs that ensure coordination among the subordinate units. Usually, each infantry battalion receives its own area of operations. Operational decisions are typically negotiated among the commanders of the national contingents, rather than being dictated by the Force Commander. Arrangements of this sort are

---

[8]IFOR is, of course, the exception, and it is appropriately controlled through NATO, not through the U.N. system.

adequate so long as the peace force is not required to conduct combat operations.

Force Commanders may also provide channels of communication for parties that are unwilling to communicate directly with each other for political reasons. For example, up to the current time, the Republic of Cyprus has refused to maintain regular contacts with Turkish Cypriot authorities to avoid the appearance of recognizing an independent state. Therefore, UNFICYP has served as an intermediary. After the 1973 Arab-Israeli War, Egypt and Syria refused to maintain continuous contacts with Israel, which might have implied its recognition. Therefore, UNEF II provided the parties with channels through which to communicate their complaints.

## MORE-AMBITIOUS OPERATIONS

In authorizing more-ambitious operations, the Security Council may invoke Chapter VI or Chapter VII. This fundamental choice has important implications for the character of the peace force.

Operating under Chapter VI, a peace force anticipates being respected as a nonbelligerent. To minimize accidental engagement, it makes itself conspicuous by wearing blue helmets and using white-painted equipment. It is usually composed of light or mechanized infantry without supporting arms and is controlled through the U.N. system.

Operating under Chapter VII, a peace force is a potential belligerent; therefore, being conspicuous serves no useful purpose. Ideally, it should be a fully capable combined-arms team and be controlled by an appropriate agent other than the U.N, but practice has been inconsistent.

In addition to military forces, more-ambitious peace operations often require a large civilian component and support from NGOs. The civilian component may include police monitors, electoral assistants, advisers, and technicians. Depending on the mandate, U.N. personnel may advise indigenous governments or they may assume administrative responsibility for an interim period. NGOs may provide critically needed humanitarian aid, including emergency health care. The responsibilities and capabilities of military forces, civilian components, and NGOs frequently overlap, making coordination important to success.

## Transition

**Capabilities.** Does the force have the required capabilities? For operations under Chapter VI, can the force defend itself while accomplishing the mandate? For operations under Chapter VII, does the force have the capabilities to accomplish its tasks against likely opposition? Is the civilian component trained and equipped to accomplish its tasks? Required capabilities vary widely, according to the situation, the tasks specified in the mandate, and whether the Security Council has invoked Chapter VI or Chapter VII.

In Namibia, the Security Council allowed a party to undertake combat operations that exceeded the capabilities of the peace force. The United Nations Transition Assistance Group (UNTAG) in Namibia was formed in 1988 to monitor the cease-fire between military forces from South Africa and the South West African People's Organization (SWAPO) and to ensure the independence of Namibia through free elections. However, with only three infantry battalions, UNTAG was unable to oppose SWAPO forces when they reentered Namibia from Angola and threatened to disrupt the peace process. In a highly unorthodox move, South African forces were allowed to act on behalf of the Security Council in repulsing SWAPO forces.

**Size.** Can the peace force attain an adequate strength within schedule? Given the situation, is it large enough to accomplish the tasks contained in the mandate?

Force size should reflect tasks to be performed, physical characteristics of the area of operations, and the time frame scheduled for the transition process. Forces deployed to implement a transition mandate have varied in size from about 1,000 for the United Nations Observer Group in Central America in Nicaragua to roughly 20,000 for UNTAC in Cambodia. ONUCA was small because the transition portion of its mandate (demobilizing the Contra guerrilla force) required just one infantry battalion to control five security zones.

Invoking Chapter VII usually implies that a large force will be required. In Haiti, for example, the Security Council initially intended to facilitate the Governors Island Agreement, concluded on July 3, 1993, between Lt. Gen. Raoul Cédras and President Jean-Bertrand Aristide, with a force of about 1,200.[9] But when the USS *Harlan County* docked in Port-au-Prince on October 11, it was confronted by violent demonstrations and departed without off-loading. In response, the Security Council invoked economic sanctions against Haiti, but the Cédras regime remained defiant.

On July 15, 1994, the Secretary-General, anticipating that the United States would lead, estimated that an operation under Chapter VII would require about 15,000 personnel.[10] On July 31, the Security Council authorized a multinational force to restore the legitimate authorities in Haiti and to permit implementation of the Governors Island Agreement. On September 19, the Multinational Force (MNF), built around the U.S. 10th Mountain Division and a Marine task force, arrived under an agreement with the Cédras regime without encountering resistance. Peak strength in early October was about 20,000 military personnel.

**Composition.** Does the composition of the peace force by national contingents ensure impartiality? Can the participating member states provide the required capabilities? Are civilian components of the operation prepared to accomplish their tasks?

As a matter of principle, no single member state is allowed to contribute more than one-third to a peace force controlled through the U.N. system. This limitation does not apply to operations conducted by member states under authorization of the Security Council, such as UNITAF in Somalia, MNF in Haiti, or the French operation in Rwanda.

---

[9]Security Council Resolution 867 on September 23, 1993, established the United Nations Mission in Haiti (UNMIH) with an authorized strength of 567 police monitors and a military construction unit with approximately 700 personnel, including 60 military trainers. It called upon the Government of Haiti to ensure safety and freedom of movement for U.N. personnel.

[10]Secretary-General Boutros-Ghali recommended a force of 5,000 combat troops and 6,500 support troops in-country, plus an offshore reserve of 3,500 troops. The civilian police component was to number about 550. He observed that forces of this size would be unobtainable through the U.N. system and recommended authorizing member states to create a multinational force. United Nations, *Report of the Secretary-General on the United Nations Mission in Haiti*, S/1994/828, July 15, 1994.

During the immediate post-colonial period, the Secretary-General did not solicit contributions from member states that had been colonial powers in the region.  This stricture is no longer observed, but national interests of these powers may cast doubt on their impartiality.  For example, France was willing to deploy troops in Rwanda (Operation Turquoise) because of its regional interests.  But exactly those interests caused complications:  The French had trained, armed, and supplied the Hutu-dominated government[11]— an association that caused misgivings in the Security Council, where five members abstained from the vote that authorized France to send troops.[12]

French troops were initially welcomed by the Hutu government but were regarded with suspicion by the Tutsi-dominated Rwandan Patriotic Front.  On July 5, 1994, after tense negotiations, the RPF endorsed French establishment of a humanitarian protection zone in southwestern Rwanda, where the Hutu-dominated government still clung to power.  At the same time, President François Mitterrand gave an assurance that France did not consider the RPF an enemy and would not oppose its eventual success.  Ten days later, the RPF routed Hutu soldiers and militiamen, who fled to Zaire.  When Operation Turquoise ended in late August, the RPF easily assumed responsibility for the protection zone.

Transition operations may be delicate and highly intrusive, requiring military contingents that are not only suitably equipped and adequately trained, but also well disciplined.  In some instances, national contingents have performed inadequately.  In Cambodia, for example, the peace force included infantry battalions from 11 coun-

---

[11]In October 1990 and again in February 1993, France sent small numbers of troops to support the Hutu-dominated government of Juvenal Habyarimana, which was confronted with RPF invasions from Uganda.  These troops served primarily as advisers to the Hutu army, helping it to assimilate and employ French arms and equipment.

[12]France asked for approval from the Security Council to ensure the security and protection of civilians at risk.  The French ambassador promised that French troops would be neutral and fire if necessary on Hutu forces.  The U.S. strongly supported the French initiative as the only practical alternative.  Rwanda, still represented by the Hutu government, and Djibouti, a country closely associated with France, voted affirmatively, while Brazil, China, Pakistan, New Zealand, and Nigeria abstained from the vote on June 22, 1994.

tries, satisfying the requirement for regional balance, and included none of the powers presumed to be partial, such as China, which was reputed to be sympathetic to the Khmer Rouge, or the United States, which had backed the Lon Nol regime. The most effective battalions were apparently those from France and the Netherlands, both former colonial powers. Reportedly, certain battalions showed little initiative, others maintained compromising relations with the PDK, and one national contingent was notoriously ill-disciplined.

**Control.** Is the peace force adequately controlled, especially given the possibility of combat? Are the military and civilian components adequately coordinated? Are there suitable arrangements for communicating with parties to the conflict? Do the contributing member states acknowledge the Special Representative and the Force Commander as the sole conduit for communicating with the parties? If the Security Council has invoked Chapter VII, is the peace force controlled by a capable agent?

Control arrangements in Cambodia were typical for a transition operation under Chapter VI. Yasushi Akashi of Japan served as Special Representative of the Secretary-General and Head of Mission. The Force Commander, Lt. Gen. John Sanderson of Australia, was subordinate to him. Supported by a small combined staff, Sanderson controlled 11 infantry battalions, each deployed in its own sector of operations.

These arrangements were adequate so long as combat operations were not undertaken. They would have been wholly inadequate had the Security Council decided to coerce the Khmer Rouge into disarming as set forth in the Paris Agreements.

## Security for Humanitarian Aid

**Capabilities.** Does the force have the required capabilities? Is it adequately prepared for self-defense while accomplishing its mandate? Can it secure humanitarian aid from entry point to final destination?

The forces of many member states lack capabilities that may be required to secure humanitarian aid. For example, motorized or mechanized infantry was required to secure humanitarian aid in Rwanda. But when the Secretary-General solicited over 50 potential contributors, only Ethiopia was prepared to contribute an appropriately equipped infantry unit.  Ghana, Malawi, Mali, Nigeria, Senegal, Zambia, Zaire, and Zimbabwe made offers on condition that their equipment requirements were met.[13]  Britain, France, and the United States offered to help equip these forces, but providing equipment and training soldiers to use it imposed delay during an acute crisis.

Lawless elements or forces controlled by the parties may attack seaports, airports, land convoys, storage facilities, and distribution centers.  In Somalia, for example, UNITAF required fire support from attack helicopters (AH-1) and mobility provided by utility helicopters (UH-60).  Attack helicopters proved especially valuable during operations in Kismayu.  There, they destroyed technical vehicles and crew-served weapons deployed by factions intent on interfering with the security operations.  UNITAF also required engineering units to construct and repair roads and bridges, as well as to clear mines.

**Size.**  Is the force large enough to secure humanitarian aid throughout the area of operations?  Is it large enough to deter parties from diverting humanitarian aid and obstructing its delivery?

If parties viewed aid from a humanitarian perspective, there would be little need to secure its delivery.  But parties usually have a political-military perspective, regarding aid as beneficial or harmful to their cause, depending on the recipients.  They construe aid to areas controlled by their opponents as aid and comfort to the enemy, and may therefore attempt to disrupt or divert its delivery.

Required force size varies according to the situation.  For example, the United Nations Interim Force in Lebanon provided some security for local villagers and farmers and for teams providing humanitarian services in the battalion sectors.  Six infantry battalions totaling some 5,000 troops were adequate for this task.[14]  But in Somalia, where security involved establishing and protecting an extensive aid-distribution system throughout a much larger area, a much larger

---

[13]United Nations, *Letter Dated 19 June 1994 from the Secretary-General Addressed to the President of the Security Council,* S/1994/728, New York, June 20, 1994.

[14]United Nations, *The Blue Helmets,* 1990, p. 144; Mona Ghali, "United Nations Interim Force in Lebanon:  1978–Present," in Durch, *The Evolution of UN Peacekeeping,* 1993, pp. 199–200.

force was required.  At peak, UNITAF included 18,000 U.S. personnel plus 14,000 troops from other states.

**Composition.**  Does the composition of the peace force by national contingents ensure impartiality?  Can the participating member states provide the required capabilities?  Security operations make greater demands than peace-keeping, so quality of the national contingents becomes increasingly important.

In Somalia during UNITAF, the peace force was dominated by the U.S. contingent, which also had operational control over Australian, Belgian, and Moroccan contingents.  This force was impartial and, with few exceptions, of extremely high quality.  By contrast, UNOSOM II was embarrassed by some military contingents that were poorly disciplined, tactically inept, or corrupt.  Canada, a country noted for distinguished support of peace operations, was embarrassed by criminal behavior of a few soldiers in its Airborne Regiment, which was later disbanded for misconduct.

**Control.**  Is the peace force adequately controlled, especially given the possibility of combat?  If the Security Council has invoked Chapter VII, has it given control to a capable agent?  Are there adequate arrangements for coordinating with U.N. agencies and NGOs involved in humanitarian aid?

In Lebanon, problems resulted from locating the UNIFIL headquarters within a sector controlled first by the occupying Israeli army and later by Israel's surrogate Lebanese force.  During the latter period, egress from the headquarters was at the sufferance of an unpredictable authority.

Coordination among U.N. agencies and NGOs can be a complex undertaking.  In Somalia, the Special Representative had to coordinate the activities of six U.N. agencies in-country.  Within UNOSOM headquarters was a Humanitarian Operations Center (HOC) that coordinated with a Civil-Military Operations Center (CMOC) operated by UNITAF.  CMOC coordinated military support for humanitarian aid either through UNOSOM II or directly with the NGOs.  This arrangement functioned well despite a cultural gap between NGO personnel, who tended to be critical of the military, and UNITAF personnel.

## Peace Enforcement

**Capabilities.** Does the force have the capabilities required to coerce recalcitrant parties at reasonable risk to itself? Depending on the situation, these capabilities may include sophisticated intelligence collection,[15] forced entry by seaborne or heliborne assault, special operations, precision strike, and logistics support for sustained combat operations.

Past attempts at peace enforcement have demonstrated that a wide range of capabilities is usually required. In the Congo, ONUC was initially at a disadvantage against foreign mercenaries, because it lacked effective communications, mobility, armored protection, and fire support.

In Somalia, UNOSOM II and U.S. forces that attempted to apprehend General Aideed lacked effective control arrangements, adequate armored protection, and artillery. In September 1993, the U.S. Forces in Somalia (USFORSOM) commander requested heavy forces. That request was refused to avoid giving an appearance of escalation and also because the need was not fully appreciated.[16] After U.S. special-

---

[15]During peace-keeping, the U.N. believes "that information, not intelligence, is the limit of what can be sought and that this should be acquired openly and shared even-handedly...." Roger H. Palin, *Multinational Military Forces: Problems and Prospects,* Oxford University Press, London, Adelphi Paper 294, 1995, p. 38. But success in peace enforcement may depend critically on intelligence acquired covertly and not shared with the parties.

[16]"The U.S. general [Maj. Gen. Thomas M. Montgomery commanding USFORSOM] previously had made clear his awareness that his 'thin-skinned' vehicles were vulnerable, and had asked for M-1A1 tanks and Bradley Fighting Vehicles, according to U.S. military sources. But that request, endorsed by the U.S. Central Command, was turned down by Defense Secretary Les Aspin. An official representing Aspin's views said that he refused the request because he got conflicting advice, saw 'no great sense of urgency,' and was sensitive to the likelihood of backlash in Congress." Barton Gellman, "Somalia Options Reviewed as Discontent in Congress Grows," *Washington Post,* October 6, 1993, p. A12. In his memoirs, General Colin Powell recalls: "I had been urging Aspin for weeks to demand a policy review to find a way out [of Somalia]. He, in turn, had been frustrated that his policy team so far had produced nothing usable. Still, with our commander on the ground pleading for help to protect American soldiers, I had to back him, as I had with the Rangers and Delta Force. With only three days left in my term [as Chairman of the Joint Chiefs of Staff], I was in Les Aspin's office making one last pitch to him to give Tom Montgomery the armor he wanted. 'It ain't gonna happen,' Aspin the political realist said. Many members of Congress, led by Senator Bob Byrd, were saying we had no further business in Somalia and should

operations forces suffered severe losses in October, the United States sent a heavy battalion task force to Mogadishu, but at the same time it terminated the hunt for Aideed.

In Bosnia-Herzegovina, UNPROFOR lacked tanks (except for a company with the Nordic Battalion), artillery, and attack helicopters. It was so deficient in ground combat power that it could not employ NATO air support effectively, either to defend itself or to accomplish its mandate. Indeed, it negated NATO air power by becoming hostage to Bosnian Serbs, most notoriously during the Srebrenica debacle.

In April 1993, the Security Council demanded that Srebrenica, a Muslim-held enclave in northeastern Bosnia, be treated as a safe area.[17] With grudging approval from the Bosnian Serbs, UNPROFOR initially deployed two Canadian companies to Srebrenica, which were subsequently relieved by a Dutch infantry battalion. The Dutch were equipped with infantry weapons and light armored vehicles, but had no artillery or tanks. To compensate for this weakness, they were authorized to request close air support from NATO. On July 6, 1995, Bosnian Serb forces began to collapse the Dutch positions by firing tank rounds near their observation posts until the Dutch felt compelled to retreat. On July 8, the Dutch commander, Lt. Col. Ton Karremans, requested close air support, but the Force Commander, Lt. Gen. Bernard Janvier of France, hesitated to approve the request, in part because the European Union envoy Carl Bildt of Sweden was in Belgrade for negotiations.[18] On the same day, Bosnian Serbs took 30 Dutch soldiers prisoner.

On July 10, NATO aircraft finally attacked two Serb tanks approaching Srebrenica, but the Serb commander, Ratko Mladic, warned

---

withdraw immediately." Colin Powell, *My American Journey*, Random House, New York, 1995, p. 586.

[17]Security Council Resolution 819, adopted on April 16, 1993, reads: "acting under Chapter VII of the Charter of the United Nations, 1. Demands that all parties and others concerned treat Srebrenica and its surroundings as a safe area which should be free from armed attack or any other hostile act; 2. Demands also to that effect the immediate cessation of armed attacks by Bosnian Serb paramilitary units against Srebrenica and their immediate withdrawal from the areas surrounding Srebrenica. . . ." The Security Council later declared five additional safe areas: Bihac, Gorazde, Sarajevo, Tuzla, and Zepa.

[18]Charles Lane, "The Fall of Srebrenica," *New Republic*, July 14, 1995, p. 14.

Karremans to stop the attacks or else he would destroy Srebrenica and kill the Dutch prisoners. Learning of these threats, Dutch Defense Minister Joris Voorhoeve requested Special Representative Yasushi Akashi of Japan not to authorize close air support. The following day, Bosnian Serb forces overran Srebrenica. Muslim women, children, and elderly people were taken by bus to the line of confrontation. Muslim men of military age attempted to flee, but thousands were massacred and buried in mass graves.[19]    On July 14, Bosnian Serbs attacked the Zepa safe area and threatened to use 65 Ukrainian soldiers as shields if NATO conducted air strikes. Bosnian President Alija Izetbegovic asked U.N. officials to negotiate for safe passage of civilians out of Zepa. Asked if this were "ethnic cleansing," Izetbegovic said: "Yes it is. But here is something worse than ethnic cleansing—ethnic killing."[20]

**Size.** Is the peace force sufficiently large to coerce recalcitrant parties and still accomplish other assigned tasks?

The peace force should be sized to accomplish its mandate against any likely opposition. Sizing calculations are analogous to those for any military campaign, with some added complications. The Force Commander might calculate that he requires fewer forces because the parties countervail each other to such an extent that no party can risk a large commitment against the peace force. Or he might calculate that he requires more forces to accomplish other tasks simultaneously, such as security for humanitarian aid.

Inadequate force size has seriously hampered past attempts at peace enforcement. When the Security Council authorized coercive action during the Congo operation, the Secretary-General's chief military

---

[19]United Nations Economic and Social Council, *Final Periodic Report on the Situation of Human Rights in the Territory of the Former Yugoslavia Submitted by Mr. Tadeusz Mazowiecki, Special Rapporteur of the Commission on Human Rights, Pursuant to Paragraph 42 of Commission Resolution 1995/89,* E/CN.4/1996/9, August 22, 1995; Michael Dobbs and Christine Spolar, "Anybody Who Moved or Screamed Was Killed; Thousands Massacred on Bosnia Trek in July," *Washington Post,* October 26, 1995, pp. A1, A24; David Rhode, "Bosnia Muslims Were Killed by the Truckload," *Christian Science Monitor,* October 2, 1995, p. 1; John Pomfret, "Gold Mine Site Adds to Indications That Missing Bosnians Are Dead," *Washington Post,* February 7, 1996, p. A15.

[20]John Pomfret, "Bosnian Serbs Claim Fall of 2nd U.N. 'Safe Area'," *Washington Post,* July 20, 1995, pp. A1, A23.

adviser calculated that ONUC would need two infantry divisions with armor and artillery support, about 40,000 men in all. But at peak strength, ONUC had half that number of troops fragmented into battalion- and company-sized national contingents. When the Security Council declared safe areas in Bosnia-Herzegovina during early 1993, the Force Commander, Lt. Gen. Jean Cot of France, estimated that 34,000 additional troops would be required to deter attacks.[21] Because member states were unwilling to contribute such large forces, the Secretary-General asked Cot to proceed with only 7,600 additional troops plus NATO air support, a size that proved to be inadequate.

**Composition.** Does the composition of the peace force by national contingents ensure impartiality? Can the participating member states provide the required capabilities? Does the composition include great powers if their participation is required for success?

Operations in Bosnia-Herzegovina raised serious questions about the impartiality of national contingents. Bosnian Serbs greeted Russian and Ukrainian contingents as allies, whereas Bosnian Muslims registered concern. Conversely, Bosnian Muslims welcomed Pakistani and Turkish contingents with enthusiasm, whereas Bosnian Serbs regarded all Muslim troops with suspicion. Inclusion of these contingents departed from U.N. tradition that member states with notorious sympathies should not contribute forces.

Successful peace enforcement on a large scale usually requires the military capabilities of great powers, and great-power leadership encourages other member states to join the operation. Of course, great-power participation does not ensure success if these powers are half-hearted in their commitment, as demonstrated in recent failures.

Operations in Somalia during 1993 depended critically on U.S. leadership and capabilities. Not only were U.S. capabilities essential, but without U.S. leadership other member states were unwilling to ac-

---

[21]According to his later statement, Maj. Gen. Lewis MacKenzie of Canada, then UNPROFOR chief of staff, thought that an additional 100,000 troops would be required to protect the safe areas. Lewis MacKenzie, "Tragic Errors," *Maclean's*, December 12, 1994, p. 35.

cept the risks of peace enforcement. Indeed, the U.S. decision to withdraw its forces impelled other European states to withdraw their forces as well. Operations in Bosnia-Herzegovina long depended on French leadership, including the large contingent of French ground forces. Had France withdrawn its forces, UNPROFOR would have ended or dwindled to insignificance.

**Control.** Is the force adequately controlled, especially given the possibility of combat? Do the arrangements ensure unity of effort? Has the Security Council given control of the peace force to a capable agent?

Prior to IFOR, inadequate control seriously hampered every attempt at peace enforcement. With this exception, the Security Council never clearly delegated control to a capable agent. In several cases, the Council attempted to mingle U.N.–control with non–U.N. control, but these hybrid arrangements proved ineffective.

The Congo operation was controlled by Special Representative Ralph J. Bunche of the United States through a Force Commander, initially Lt. Gen. Carl C. von Horn of Sweden. At peak, the Force Commander controlled contingents from 28 participating states, an unwieldy span of control. The operation was launched without preliminary planning or coordination, and units were scattered across the Congo before adequate communications were available. To further complicate the situation, the U.N. representative in Katanga, Conor Cruise O'Brien of Ireland, interpreted the mandate differently from authorities in Leopoldville (Kinshasa) or New York. Success in Katanga was ultimately owed to an Indian brigade controlled through national channels.

In mid-1993, the Somalia operation was controlled through U.N. channels and through unilateral U.S. channels. The U.N. channel extended from the Secretary-General to SRSG Admiral Jonathan T. Howe of the United States and then to the Force Commander Lt. Gen. Çevik Bir of Turkey. Bir had only the weak authority traditionally accorded a Force Commander. He had to solicit assent for operational decisions from the national contingents—in effect, negotiating his operational plans. Bir's deputy commander, Maj. Gen. Thomas Montgomery of the United States, was simultaneously the commander of most U.S. forces in Somalia, but these forces were not assigned to UNOSOM II. In addition, Maj. Gen. William F. Garrison commanded special-operations forces in a chain of command that extended through USCENTCOM without involving either Montgomery or Bir. These control arrangements remained workable only through personal relationships; they were inadequate for combat operations.[22]

---

[22]"*However, there should be no mistaking the fact that the greatest obstacles to unity of command during UNOSOM II were imposed by the United States on itself.* Especially at the end of the operations, these command arrangements had effectively created a condition that allowed no one to set clear, unambiguous priorities in designing and executing a comprehensive force package." Kenneth Allard, *Somalia Operations: Lessons Learned,* National Defense University Press, Washington, D.C., 1995, p. 60. Emphasis in the original text.

# Chapter Seven

# PHYSICAL ENVIRONMENT

How will the physical environment affect the operation? Peace operations have taken place in some of the world's most inhospitable, rugged, and densely forested terrain, greatly impeding operations. The physical environment affects peace operations across the spectrum, but the specific effects vary according to the type of operation.

What effects will climate and terrain have on the operation? How will the availability of infrastructure, such as airports, seaports, and road networks, affect it? What facilities will the parties make available? What facilities must be constructed, improved, or repaired?

## PEACE-KEEPING

### Observation

**Climate and Terrain.** What problems will climate and terrain pose for observers? What obstacles impede clear and continuous observation? Do conditions require the use of certain equipment, such as rotary-wing aircraft?

Rugged terrain, inclement weather, and heavy vegetation often hinder observers from accomplishing their mandate. For example, hilly, rocky terrain can mask the observers' field of view and prevent access to better points of ground observation. Blowing sand or driving, monsoon-like rains can have similarly degrading effects. Heavy weather and habitually low-hanging clouds can also prevent regular use of observer aircraft. Heavy vegetation, particularly in tropical and subtropical areas, can prevent observation of troop and vehicular movement.

**Infrastructure.** How will availability of airfields, seaports, roads, railroads, shelter, and local sources of supply affect observation? Will special equipment be required to ensure successful observation? Lack of infrastructure increases the expense and difficulty of the operation. It may also limit the observers' effectiveness, even when they have been provided with suitable vehicles and aircraft.

Areas of operations have included countries such as Afghanistan, Angola, Kashmir, and Yemen, where little infrastructure was available. In addition, available infrastructure may be severely degraded and damaged by the conflict. In extreme cases, observers may have to provide their own transport, sustaining supplies, shelter, and communications gear. For example, UNAVEM I had to contend with roads that were sparse, poorly maintained, and sown with land mines. Food and water were contaminated by disease, and most of the country was without telephone service.

## Interposition

**Climate and Terrain.** How will climate and terrain affect the operation? Is the buffer zone bordered by definite terrain features? To what extent will rough terrain and vegetation affect the ability of the interposition force to detect violations? Will prevailing weather limit surveillance and mobility? What urban areas included in the buffer zone will require special consideration?

Terrain features that define the buffer zone and low population densities tend to facilitate interposition operations. For example, the Suez Canal and Sinai Desert facilitated interposition between Egyptian and Israeli forces. The Golan Heights merge gradually into the Syrian Plain and are dotted with villages that cause contortions in the buffer zone or lie within it, yet still constitute a reasonably compact and sparsely populated area.

A greater contrast is presented by the buffer zone in Cyprus, which follows a tortuous course that does not correspond to consistent terrain features. Where the buffer zone passes through the city of Nicosia ("Green Line"), it becomes only a few yards wide.

The buffer zone in Croatia meandered through rough and heavily forested terrain, making control extremely difficult.

**Infrastructure.** How will interposition be affected by the availability of airfields, seaports, roads, railroads, shelter, and local sources of supply?

Operations in Cyprus were greatly facilitated by the infrastructure available in two Sovereign Base Areas (Akrotiri and Dhekelia) retained by Britain under the Treaty of Alliance signed in 1960. Britain made these bases available to UNFICYP and provided logistics support units. The current buffer zone is anchored at its eastern end on the Dhekelia Sovereign Base Area.[1]

## MORE-AMBITIOUS OPERATIONS

### Transition

**Climate and Terrain.** How will climate and terrain affect the operation? Transition operations often require close and frequent interaction among the civilian and military components of the peace force scattered throughout the country. What effects will terrain have on the civilian component of the operation?

In Cambodia, terrain greatly impeded all aspects of the operation. Much of central Cambodia is low-lying, poorly drained, and swampy; the western and northern parts of the country contain wide expanses of forest and jungle. These features impeded the initial deployment and subsequent interaction of UNTAC components, especially since much of the force did not arrive until after the onset of the monsoon season. In addition, Cambodian terrain favored unconventional forces, primarily the Khmer Rouge but also bandits, who could conceal themselves in the jungles and swamps. UNTAC was further impeded by man-made obstacles: thousands of land mines sown during a decade of war.

---

[1] "Sovereign Base Area" is a legal term used in the treaty with Britain signed when the Republic of Cyprus was created. Britain has sovereign rights i.e., unlimited, within these base areas, as though they were British territory.

**Infrastructure.** How will availability of airfields, seaports, roads, railroads, shelter, and local sources of supply affect the operation? Are the airports and seaports adequate to receive the civilian and military components of the force? How accessible is the area of interest by road transport? What airfields will accept fixed-wing aircraft or rotary-wing aircraft? Are available communications facilities adequate?

In Cambodia, UNTAC's dependence on a poorly developed road network was offset by frequent use of the country's four major airports, each in a different administrative region. In Nicaragua, under comparable road conditions, ONUCA was able to disarm and demobilize the Contras only because they proceeded willingly, often on foot, to five prearranged security zones.[2] ONUCA depended heavily on Canadian military and commercially leased helicopters to conduct regular patrols and to deliver supplies into these zones.[3]

## Security for Humanitarian Aid

**Climate and Terrain.** What effects will climate and terrain have on the peace force's ability to secure humanitarian aid?

Climate and terrain can heavily influence operations to secure humanitarian aid. In Somalia, for example, security operations were hampered by enervating heat and by a sprawling urban environment that was difficult to oversee and control. In Lebanon, the ability of UNIFIL to prevent sporadic attacks by armed bands was constrained by terrain interlaced with winding ravines offering concealment.[4]

**Infrastructure.** How will available infrastructure affect the operation? How well will the available infrastructure support initial deployment? Will the force have to construct or improve airports and seaports? How well will available transportation support delivery of aid to the afflicted populations?

---

[2]"Security zone" was the term used in the mandate; it implied that ONUCA would ensure the security of demobilizing Contras, i.e., they would not be attacked or arrested.

[3]Durch, *The Evolution of UN Peacekeeping*, 1993, pp. 446, 449–450.

[4]United Nations, *The Blue Helmets*, 1990, pp. 126–129.

Deployment to Somalia was severely hampered by lack of adequate airports, seaports, and roads. Airlift into southern Somalia was constrained by the availability of only four airfields: Baidoa, Baledogle, Kismayu, and Mogadishu. Of these, only Kismayu and Mogadishu could accommodate more than one cargo aircraft on the ground at a time, and only Mogadishu could accept C-5 aircraft. Sealift into southern Somalia was limited to the two seaports at Kismayu and Mogadishu, seaports that were in poor repair, lacked lighterage, had no deep berths, and offered little sheltered anchorage. Movement within Somalia was hampered by deteriorating roads, destroyed bridges, and land mines.

## Peace Enforcement

**Climate and Terrain.** What effects will climate and terrain have on military operations? Do they tend to favor particular types of forces? Would they offer significant advantages to recalcitrant parties opposing the peace force? What strategy and tactics would be advantageous in this environment?

Like all combat operations, peace enforcement is strongly affected by climate and terrain. In Somalia, the oppressively hot climate and dearth of potable water enervated troops and constrained their operations. Urban terrain also constrained combat. Combat was concentrated in a few urban areas, especially the seaports (Berbera, Kismayu, Mogadishu), and villages located in the southern half of the interior. The urban terrain of Mogadishu, a maze of tin-roofed shacks and some masonry structures, had the greatest effect on operations, because it favored local militias by allowing them to concentrate and disperse at will, and to ambush conventional forces. During the October 1993 fighting, the U.S. rapid-reaction force, mounted in light vehicles, failed to penetrate sections of Mogadishu held by Aideed's followers.

The terrain in central Bosnia-Herzegovina is ideally suited to militias and irregular forces. In fact, this mountainous, heavily forested terrain was the setting for the most celebrated and successful guerrilla fighting of WWII. It offers excellent concealment and many opportunities for raids and ambushes. In addition, the climate tends to favor irregular forces: Frequent storms and cloud cover impede air operations, especially ground attack missions. In winter, snowfall and ice stall traffic, especially on the winding mountain roads.

**Infrastructure.** How will the availability of airfields, seaports, roads, railroads, shelter, and local sources of supply affect operations? What throughput can be anticipated using available airports and seaports? How well will the transportation net support deployment and supply? What improvements would be required to sustain large forces engaged in protracted combat operations?

Inadequate infrastructure in Somalia slowed the pace of U.N. and U.S. operations while increasing their cost. Somalia's poorly developed seaports delayed or prevented off-loading of prepositioned ships. Its few airstrips had almost no support facilities. Its roads and bridges were in extremely poor repair. Its lack of resources compelled multilateral forces to import almost every item of supply, including, in many cases, their drinking water, and increased the need for tactical airlift, especially transport helicopters.

In contrast, the former Yugoslavia has well-developed seaports, modern airports, a railway system, and a network of all-weather roads. Even Bosnia-Herzegovina, although less well developed than Slovenia or Croatia, has fairly extensive and modern infrastructure. Operating from its logistics base at Split, UNPROFOR could supply its units by road convoy, unless the Bosnian Serbs blocked passage. However, UNPROFOR accomplished primarily noncombat tasks, which made low demands on supply.

Sustaining IFOR, a force prepared for combat operations, required that the infrastructure be improved. To establish a line of communication through Hungary, the United States decided to bridge the Sava River. After a setback due to flooding, U.S. combat engineers successfully deployed approximately 600 yards of pontoon bridging across the swollen river. In addition, U.S. forces rapidly established flight operations at several airports by deploying ground control equipment and repairing runways and hardstands.[5]

---

[5]A *hardstand* is ground prepared for use by aircraft and associated ground vehicles to unload aircraft and store materiel. At a fully developed airport, it is usually concrete, but at field sites it might be pierced steel planking or another less-permanent expedient.

# Chapter Eight

# EXTENT OF INTERNATIONAL SUPPORT

Will states that are not parties adequately support the operation? *Support* includes voting affirmatively, participating in the operation, and applying political pressure on the parties to keep their agreements.

Some states, exemplified by Canada and the Scandinavian countries, participate in traditional peace-keeping because they are morally and ideologically committed to the principles of the Charter. In addition, some states view peace-keeping as a way to increase their prestige and improve relations with great powers. But motives that suffice for peace-keeping may not be adequate for Chapter VII operations, including peace enforcement, with their inherent risk of casualties. To participate in such operations, states may have to believe that their geopolitical interests justify such a high level of involvement. For example, U.S. willingness to lead IFOR is heavily conditioned by the U.S. role in NATO and U.S. concern with the stability of Eastern Europe. A further tension underlies peace operations at the high end: Participating states must have enough interest to justify the monetary cost and risk to their troops, yet be sufficiently disinterested to maintain impartiality.

Critical issues include support from the five permanent members of the Security Council, the United States as a national actor, and regional powers that have political influence on the parties. In all cases, the Permanent Five must be willing to approve the mandate; at the high end of peace operations, they also must generate a robust consensus for action. Discord among the Permanent Five can cause protracted frustration, as was demonstrated in the Congo and, more recently, in Bosnia-Herzegovina.  U.S. participation, discussed broadly in Chapter Two, is always critical for peace enforcement and, sometimes, also for less-demanding operations.  Finally, regional powers often exert strong influence on peace operations by supporting sanctions, especially arms embargoes, and by keeping political pressure on the parties to stay within the peace process.

## PEACE-KEEPING

A *community of interest*, implying mere approval or acquiescence of the Permanent Five, is often sufficient to support peace-keeping.

### Observation

**Permanent Five.**  Is the community of interest sufficiently robust? What events might cause any of the Permanent Five to withdraw support?  To what extent does success depend on support from great powers other than the United States?

For example, the Soviet Union assented to the Second United Nations Emergency Force in 1973 because it wanted to shield Egypt from further Israeli advances.  But it blocked a new mandate in 1979, because of a shift in international politics.

In 1973, Egypt had been a Soviet client—indeed, the Soviet Union's most important ally in the Arab world.  But in 1976, Egypt terminated its Treaty of Friendship with the Soviet Union and turned toward the United States.  In March 1979, Egypt and Israel signed a treaty negotiated at Camp David through President Jimmy Carter's mediation.  Under Article VI of this treaty, Israel agreed to withdraw from the Sinai peninsula, and the parties requested the U.N. to observe the demilitarized zone and to monitor freedom of navigation in the Strait of Tiran.  In an annex, the United States offered to organize a multilateral peace force if the U.N. were unable to perform those functions.  As anticipated, the Soviet Union sided with Arab states opposed to Camp David and refused to authorize a U.N. observer force to monitor compliance with the treaty, compelling the United States to sponsor a Sinai observer force outside the U.N. system.

**United States.** Is U.S. participation required? Do U.S. interests justify its participation? Should the United States participate in the observer force? If so, under what circumstances should U.S. participation be terminated?

Observers need broad military experience and the skills of a mediator, plus commitment to impartiality. Any member state that maintains a professional military establishment can provide such officers. As a general rule, the Secretary-General has preferred member states other than the Permanent Five and, of course, has excluded states believed to be partial.

But the United States has participated in observer forces to demonstrate its concern and to exert influence on the parties. For example, the United States continually participated in UNTSO in the Near East and was an early participant in the United Nations Military Observer Force in India and Pakistan. It currently contributes to UNPREDEP, a "preventive deployment" intended to deter violations of the Macedonian border, violations that could widen the conflict in former Yugoslavia.

**Regional Powers.** Will regional powers adequately support the mandate? Are there regional powers whose assistance is crucial to success? If so, how firm and reliable is their support?

Support from regional powers can be crucial. For example, the United Nations Observer Group in Lebanon was mandated to ensure that there was no illegal infiltration of personnel or supply of arms across the Lebanese borders, especially the land border with Syria. The United Arab Republic (Egypt and Syria) was suspected of aiding insurgents within Lebanon, but denied these allegations and refused to assist UNOGIL, compelling it to deploy exclusively in Lebanon. Moreover, Lebanese opposition groups initially prevented UNOGIL from moving freely around the country.

## Interposition

**Permanent Five.** Is the community of interest sufficiently robust? What community of interest is required among the Permanent Five? What events might cause any of these powers to withdraw support?

To what extent does success depend on support from great powers other than the United States?

Because of Cold War rivalry, the community of interest was insufficient to make UNOGIL successful. When civil war broke out in Lebanon during 1958, Lebanon and Jordan felt threatened by the newly created United Arab Republic. The United States and Britain supported Lebanon and Jordan while the Soviet Union supported the United Arab Republic. The Soviet Union allowed creation of UNOGIL—probably because it did not want the question referred to the General Assembly, then dominated by pro-Western states—but the Soviets defeated a U.S. initiative to establish UNOGIL as an interposition force. Invited by the Lebanese government, the United States landed forces in Beirut during July, but withdrew in October when the government had reestablished its authority.

**United States.** Is U.S. participation required? Do U.S. interests justify its participation? Are there special political reasons for the United States to participate? If so, under what circumstances should U.S. participation be terminated? Is there domestic and congressional support for U.S. participation or could it be marshaled?

The United States has seldom contributed to an interposition force. It often has interests that mitigate against impartiality, and it may want to avoid operations that are likely to become interminable. In addition, U.S. prestige could be diminished by interposing U.S. troops between two stronger forces.

But in some circumstances, the United States may believe that its participation would be required. For example, the United States has agreed to consider deploying forces on the Golan Heights to monitor a buffer zone between Israel and Syria following some future peace agreement, analogous to U.S. operations on the Sinai peninsula. Israeli officials claim that U.S. participation is required to assure Israelis that it is safe to relinquish the Heights.[1] Some U.S. critics

---

[1]However, the chairman of the Likud Party and current President, Benjamin Netanyahu, offered this argument against U.S. deployment: "The same terrorists now striking at innocent Israelis would relish a chance to kill Americans instead, particularly if doing so could humiliate the United States by compelling it—as in Beirut and Somalia—to withdraw under fire. A small, lightly armed U.S. deployment would be no barrier to either a terrorist or a full-fledged Syrian attack and thus would not provide

argue that the United States would be placed in a false position, ostensibly neutral yet actually pro-Israel, while offering a temptation to terrorists.

**Regional Powers.** So far as their help is required, will regional powers adequately support the mandate? Do regional powers believe that the mandate is compatible with their interests? Will they help to accomplish the mandate? Are there regional powers whose policies might diminish the chances for success?

Regional powers may support interposition to promote regional stability. They may also exert political or economic leverage on the parties to maintain their agreements. For example, Germany has tried to moderate Croatian policy during the protracted conflict in the former Yugoslavia. Regional powers may also be especially appropriate participants in the interposition force. For example, participants in UNCRO included Belgium, Denmark, Czechoslovakia, and Poland—regional states interested in resolving the conflict in the former Yugoslavia.

## MORE-AMBITIOUS OPERATIONS

More-ambitious peace operations, especially operations under Chapter VII, may require *consensus for action*—analogous to an alliance—among the Permanent Five, not merely a community of interest.

### Transition

**Permanent Five.** Is the consensus for action sufficiently robust? Is the mandate sufficiently compatible with the interests of the Permanent Five to ensure their continuing support? What divergence of interest underlies formal approval? What impact might this divergence have on the operation?

---

the crucial security required to preserve the peace. It could, however, greatly complicate Israel's ability to take preemptive military actions necessary for its defense in case of an incipient attack by Syria." Benjamin Netanyahu, "Two Keys to Mideast Peace," *Washington Post*, February 24, 1995, p. A21.

During the Cold War, the Permanent Five could seldom agree on more-ambitious operations.  When they did agree, they were likely to be at cross-purposes—for example, during the Cyprus operation. The Soviet Union approved the UNFICYP mandate to "contribute to the maintenance and restoration of law and order and a return to normal conditions" because it wished to forestall NATO intervention, but the Soviet Union refused to pay an assessment for the operation. During outbreaks of violence that frustrated transition to "normal conditions," the Soviets favored the government of Cyprus, although its National Guard was frequently responsible for precipitating incidents.  In this case, one of the Permanent Five approved a mandate for its own reasons, without fully supporting it.

**United States.**  Is U.S. participation required?  Are unique U.S. capabilities or leadership required for success?  Are U.S. interests sufficiently strong to justify this participation?  How would U.S. interests be affected if the operation failed?  Is there domestic and congressional support for U.S. participation or could it be marshaled?

Recent experience, particularly in Somalia, Haiti, and Bosnia-Herzegovina, strongly suggests that U.S. participation is the *sine qua non* for successful peace operations under Chapter VII, especially if peace enforcement becomes necessary.  An ambitious attempt to enforce peace in Somalia failed completely when the United States withdrew its forces.  There would have been no operation in Haiti had the United States not dislodged the Cédras regime by threatening to invade.

Peace operations in Bosnia-Herzegovina were costly and humiliating failures until the United States brokered the Dayton Agreements and deployed its forces to enforce them.

In all these cases, the level of U.S. interest and commitment was critical.  The United States left Somalia because its commitment would not sustain even a tactical reverse.  It took a strong interest in Haiti only when inundated by refugees fleeing the military regime. Because of disinterest, the United States long refused to deploy troops in Bosnia-Herzegovina although its NATO allies were heavily involved.

IFOR illustrates in dramatic fashion the crucial importance of U.S. participation.  Despite invocation of Chapter VII, participation by three great powers (Britain, France, Russia), deployment of large ground forces, extensive air support, and intense diplomatic activity on many levels, peace operations failed until the United States decided to participate. In the wake of successful Croat-Muslim offensives and punitive air strikes against Bosnian Serb targets, the United States succeeded in mediating peace agreements that included provisions to enforce the peace if necessary. In the Dayton Agreements, the parties consented to deployment of a peace force that would be directed against themselves if they failed to fulfill their agreements. Acting under Chapter VII, the Security Council subsequently authorized member states to create IFOR.[2]

Despite widespread skepticism and much outright opposition in Congress, the Clinton Administration gained approval for U.S. participation in IFOR.[3] IFOR assumed control over two-thirds of UNPROFOR military units then in-country,[4] yet it was a radically different force. Unlike its hapless predecessor, IFOR was explicitly prepared for combat and it included the greater part of a U.S. heavy division. In dramatic contrast to their previous behavior, all parties treated IFOR with respect and fulfilled their agreements to cease fire and to withdraw from a narrow buffer zone. It appears very unlikely that the same result could have been achieved without U.S. participation.

---

[2]On December 15, 1995, the Security Council passed Resolution 1031, welcoming signature of the General Framework Agreement based on the Dayton Agreements and authorizing member states to establish IFOR. This resolution states the essential principle of a transition operation under Chapter VII as follows: "stresses that the parties shall be held equally responsible for compliance with that Annex [1-A of the Peace Agreement], and shall be equally subject to such enforcement action by IFOR as may be necessary to ensure implementation of that Annex and the protection of IFOR and takes note that the parties have consented to IFOR's taking such measures."

[3]On December 13, 1995, the U.S. Senate voted for U.S. participation on the grounds that "preserving United States credibility is a strategic interest" while setting a one-year time limit. Thereafter, the House of Representatives dropped by a narrow margin (218 to 210) its earlier resolution, which would have denied funding, reluctantly assenting to the Senate's position.

[4]Control over the civilian component of the U.N. mission was assumed by the United Nations Mission in Bosnia and Herzegovina (UNMIBH). UNMIBH assumed responsibility for an International Police Task Force, a Mine Action Center, and civil affairs officers.

**Regional Powers.** So far as their help is required, will regional powers adequately support the mandate? What interests of regional powers are affected by the transition? In what ways might regional powers impede or promote the transition? How might they be encouraged to give their support?

The interests of regional states may be directly affected by a transition operation, in turn affecting their support. For example, the transition in Cambodia elicited different reactions from Thailand and Vietnam, both signatories to the Paris Agreement. Eager to divest itself of an onerous responsibility, Vietnam supported the operation by refraining from further intervention, despite concern over the fate of Vietnamese settlers in Cambodia. In contrast, Thailand was motivated by economic gain and a well-founded fear that the PDK might cross the border into Thailand. It hindered the peace operation by trading with the PDK.

## Security for Humanitarian Aid

**Permanent Five.** Is the consensus for action sufficiently robust? The Permanent Five are affected by circumstances and by political considerations, as well as by the extent of human suffering. For example, both Rwanda and Somalia experienced catastrophic suffering, but responses were very different. For Somalia, the Permanent Five approved not only the U.S.–led UNITAF but also a large successor operation (UNOSOM II), with participation by Britain and France. Owing in part to failures in Somalia, the Permanent Five carefully limited their involvement in Rwanda, thus discouraging participation by other states.

**United States.** Is U.S. participation and leadership required to ensure success? Could any other state or coalition perform the same functions? Do U.S. interests justify its participation? If the United States does participate, how could it avoid deeper involvement in the crisis? Conversely, what deeper involvement would be justified by U.S. interests? Is there domestic and congressional support for U.S. participation, or can it be marshaled?

Not just participation but U.S. leadership was crucial to secure humanitarian aid in Somalia. The four-battalion force planned for UNOSOM I might have secured arrival at the seaports, but not distribution throughout the country, where distribution would have been on sufferance of faction leaders intent on promoting their own power. Some aid would have trickled down to victims while much aid bolstered leaders intent on continuing the conflict, a phenomenon later observed at the refugee camps in Zaire. Under these circumstances, U.S. participation was required for success.

**Regional Powers.** So far as their help is required, will regional powers adequately support the mandate? What leverage might regional powers exert on the parties? What resources might regional powers contribute to the operation? To what extent will the operation require use of their territory?

Regional powers may support security operations to prevent or contain refugee flows that threaten their own stability. For example, UNOSOM II was adequately supported by regional powers, especially Ethiopia, which hosted peace conferences, and Kenya, which provided facilities for the American airlift. But these powers had very little direct influence on the faction leaders. UNAMIR required support from Zaire, where the majority of Hutu refugees had fled to escape from the new Tutsi-dominated government of Rwanda.

## Peace Enforcement

**Permanent Five.** Is the consensus for action sufficiently robust? Can the Permanent Five agree on desired outcome and strategy? Are they determined to bring the operation to a successful conclusion? What divergence of interest is concealed beneath formal approval? How might this divergence disrupt the operation or lessen its chance of success?

Peace enforcement requires a robust consensus for action among the Permanent Five concerning scope and purpose—a consensus that has often been fragile or absent. France and Russia reluctantly approved the Congo operation and subsequently refused to pay for it. The Permanent Five solidly approved peace enforcement in Somalia, but on the understanding that the United States would lead, requiring minimal support from other great powers.

There were widely divergent views on Bosnia-Herzegovina. Russia was sympathetic to its traditional Serb ally; the United States took an opposite view, considering Serb aggression the primary cause of the war. France and most other European countries were critical of Bosnian Serbs, but held all parties responsible for the conflict. Such divergent views precluded a consensus for action and led to ambiguity and confusion on an operational level.

**United States.** Is U.S. participation required? Do U.S. interests justify its participation? Does the United States have strong geopolitical or economic interests, treaty commitments, or special strategic concerns that justify its participation? Are U.S. participation and leadership crucial to success? Under what circumstances should the United States terminate its participation? Would U.S. withdrawal cause the operation to fail? Is there domestic and congressional support for U.S. participation or can it be marshaled?

These questions should be posed before the United States votes to invoke Chapter VII—not *after* a party becomes defiant, when it may be too late. Whenever a party becomes uncooperative during a Chapter VII peace operation, the Security Council must either enforce its will or accept loss of prestige. During the past several years, especially in Liberia, Somalia, and Bosnia-Herzegovina, the Security Council has failed to enforce peace when the United States has refused to participate or has participated in desultory fashion, even if several other great powers had contributed forces. In view of this record, the United States should carefully weigh every invocation of Chapter VII as potential peace enforcement that might require U.S. participation to succeed.

**Regional Powers.** So far as their help is required, will regional powers adequately support the mandate? Do regional powers believe that peace enforcement is compatible with their interests? To what extent will they adopt policies and take actions that will increase the chances of success?

Regional powers may participate, contribute resources, and exert political influence on the parties. For example, during the Congo operation, the non-aligned regional states tended to support the Marxist direction of Patrice Lumumba and to demand the recovery of Katanga. President Kwame Nkrumah of Ghana strongly supported Lumumba, leading to clashes between the Ghanaian contingent and anti-Lumumba forces.

When Prime Minister Lumumba was murdered in Katanga, countries supporting him, including Guinea, Mali, Morocco, and the United Arab Republic, withdrew their troops from ONUC, causing a sudden decline in strength at a critical moment. Former French colonies in Africa, such as the Congo (Brazzaville) and the Central African Republic, were encouraged by France's obstructionist policies and openly opposed enforcement. In these circumstances, India played a crucial role. Prime Minister Jawaharal Nehru of India opposed the Katangan regime because he considered it neo-colonial and, hence, was willing to order the Indian brigade to suppress the Katangan secession—the one important success during the Congo operation.

# Chapter Nine

# CONCLUSION

Since the end of the Cold War, the Security Council has authorized more-extensive and more-ambitious peace operations, including several efforts at peace enforcement. While conducting these operations, the Council has suffered spectacular and humiliating failures that have overshadowed successes in lesser peace operations and eroded the prestige of the Security Council. To prevent recurrence of such failures and recover prestige, the Council should resolve the issues presented in this report.

The Security Council should carefully judge the stage of conflict and not try to conduct peace operations when the parties do not want peace. It should hold parties to their word and not obscure the central issue of consent by allowing them to maintain a pretense. It should ensure that mandates are feasible, especially considering the peace force. Most important, it should make operations consonant with the political will of its own members. The United States cannot effect these reforms alone, but as the leading state it bears the greatest share of responsibility.

## JUDGING THE STAGE OF CONFLICT

Peace operations, even those conducted under Chapter VII, presuppose that the conflict has reached a stage that the parties believe is conclusive. If, to the contrary, parties believe that they can still advance their interests by fighting, then even a successful Chapter VII operation can gain only momentary respite. Too frequently, the Security Council has launched or continued peace operations despite strong indications that the parties intended to go on fighting.

In Lebanon, the hapless peace force is largely irrelevant to a protracted conflict between Hezbollah and Israeli forces. Somalia is still not ripe for any peace operation short of forcible disarmament of the warring clans. The factions in Liberia are fighting primarily for loot and seem to regard the international community as an additional victim to plunder. The conflict in the former Yugoslavia was little amenable to peace operations until the Croats had attained most of their war aims and the Bosnian Serbs had suffered reverses; in other words, the conflict had reached a culminating point.

Admittedly, there are strong pressures on the Security Council to continue even those operations that have long been failing. Member states initiate peace operations because they feel that something should be done. To terminate operations while the conflict is still raging implies that nothing can be done, that the Council has decided to leave not just the parties but peoples to their fate. Very often, terminating peace operations will also diminish the ability of non-governmental agencies to deliver humanitarian aid.

Given these conflicting motives, it is not surprising that each new agreement among the parties nourishes hope that a turning point may still be reached. But if the Security Council is to regain prestige, it must be quicker to recognize when conflicts are not amenable to peace operations and decline to authorize them. The United States should help to instill this more realistic outlook.

## HOLDING PARTIES TO THEIR WORD

The issue of consent is central to all peace operations and should not be obscured by allowing parties to offer a pretense of consent while they actually subvert the mandate. Of course, actual consent is likely to fall short of the formal consent manifested in agreements. It would be unrealistic to expect that parties, especially those involved in civil conflict, would maintain the precise letter of their agreements. On the contrary, most parties will usually try to twist agreements in ways favorable to themselves and commit violations. But at some point, the Security Council must hold the parties to their word or risk humiliation.

It is especially important that the Council draw a clear line between consent and recalcitrance. At a minimum, attacking the peace force or holding its personnel hostage should be regarded as evidence that a party does not support the mandate, with important consequences for the peace operation. So long as the parties maintain their consent to the operation, the peace force should expect to be treated as a nonbelligerent, as symbolized by blue helmets.

When any party becomes recalcitrant, blue helmets serve no useful purpose; indeed, they are worse than useless. The worst failures, especially in Bosnia-Herzegovina, Croatia, Liberia, and Somalia, have occurred because the Council accepted a pretense of consent from parties who did not actually support the mandate. In several instances, most lamentably in Bosnia-Herzegovina, the Council allowed peace forces to operate in a confusing twilight zone, ostensibly with consent and actually at the mercy of recalcitrant parties. Whether or not its own troops participate, the United States should insist that parties be held to their word.

## ENSURING THAT MANDATES ARE FEASIBLE

When framing mandates, the Security Council should carefully evaluate their feasibility, especially considering the limited forces that member states are usually willing to contribute. Too often, the Council has issued mandates that overtaxed the peace force, even though permanent members of the Council participated. To be taken seriously by belligerent parties, the Council must ensure that its words do not outrun its deeds. For example, during the Rwanda crisis in April 1994, the United States helped ensure that the Council avoided mandates that were not feasible, despite political pressures to take a more active role.

The Security Council lacks immediate access to a military staff that could plan large-scale (multi-battalion) peace operations and estimate the required forces. Indeed, it is doubtful whether such a staff should be created within the United Nations system, even assuming that there were support for the proposal. Therefore, whenever large-scale operations are contemplated, the Council should turn to an outside agent—for example, NATO in the case of IFOR. Considering its historical role in peace operations and its unrivaled military power, the United States is most likely to take the lead in this planning, unilaterally, within NATO, or as leader of an ad hoc coalition.

## MAKING OPERATIONS CONSONANT WITH POLITICAL WILL

Most important, the Security Council should make peace operations consonant with the political will of member states, especially its own permanent members.  It seems strange that permanent members would pass resolutions exceeding their political will, but undeniably they have done so, most notoriously in the former Yugoslavia.  There is an enormous gap between the potential power of the Council, essentially perpetuating the victorious alliance of WWII, and its actual power, which may be negligible.  To realize its potential power, the Council must generate a consensus for action that reflects the political will of its members.  Absent such consensus, the Council becomes powerless and its resolutions—mere exhortations that the parties can defy without ill consequences to themselves—command no more respect than those of the General Assembly.

Within the Security Council, the United States is primus inter pares whose policy is often essential to building consensus.  Its leading role is especially apparent in Chapter VII operations, whether or not they ultimately entail peace enforcement.  No other state could have led Chapter VII peace operations in Africa (Somalia), the Western Hemisphere (Haiti), and Europe (Bosnia-Herzegovina).  When the United States supports an operation, especially through its own participation, other member states are drawn into the endeavor.  When the United States displays disinterest or irresolution, no other state can repair the lack.

It is unrealistic to expect that some nebulous entity such as the international community will be able to conduct Chapter VII operations successfully.  For such operations, the United States should expect to lead other willing states as it has done in cases of enforcement against aggressors.  If the United States itself lacks political will or cannot elicit enough support, it should prevent the Council from invoking Chapter VII, rather than approve peace operations that are likely to fail and further discredit the Council.

# TERMS USED IN THIS REPORT

This appendix provides definitions for terms used in the report.

**Chapter VI:** (1) Articles 33 through 38 of the Charter of the United Nations, concerning the pacific settlement of disputes; (2) authority conferred by the Security Council to employ lethal force in self-defense while accomplishing a mandate.

**Chapter VII:** (1) Articles 39 through 51 of the Charter of the United Nations, concerning action with respect to threats to the peace, breaches of the peace, and acts of aggression; (2) authority conferred by the Security Council to employ lethal force beyond self-defense to accomplish a mandate.

**Combined:** Inclusion of more than one state, e.g., the United States, France, and Britain. (American military usage)

**Command:** "The authority that a commander in the Military Service lawfully exercises over subordinates by virtue of rank or assignment." (Joint Chiefs of Staff, 1994, p. 78) "No President has ever relinquished command over U.S. forces. Command constitutes the authority to issue orders covering every aspect of military operations and administration. The sole source of legitimacy for U.S. commanders originates from the U.S. Constitution, federal law and the Uniform Code of Military Justice and flows from the President to the lowest U.S. commander in the field.[1] The chain of command from the

---

[1]The qualifying phrase "in the field" is puzzling. Command is exerted in garrison and during a movement, as well as in the field. In the United States Army, the lowest echelon of command is company, battery, troop, or separate detachment.

President to the lowest commander in the field remains inviolate."[2] (U.S. Department of State, 1994, p. 10)

**Conflict:** Deliberate, organized use of lethal force, at a level exceeding terrorism, to attain political aims.

**Consensus for action:** The Permanent Five and other involved states share an understanding of what outcome is desirable, how that outcome can be achieved, what effort is required, and which states will sustain that effort.

**Consent:** The evident willingness of parties, so far as they exist, to help accomplish a mandate. In the absence of parties, consent might be given by a legitimate government. Formal consent is manifested in statements, declarations, accords, agreements, etc. Actual consent is apparent from the behavior of the parties in the course of a peace operation. *Consent* is a complex phenomenon affected by the parties' aims, the balance of power, influence of other powers, and the effectiveness of peace operations, among other factors.

**Control:** "Authority which may be less than full command exercised by a commander over part of the activities of subordinate or other organizations." (Joint Chiefs of Staff, 1994, p. 90)

**Diplomacy:** (1) Conduct of relations among sovereign states by their heads or accredited representatives, (2) activities listed under Chapter VI, Article 33 of the Charter of the United Nations: negotiation, inquiry, mediation, conciliation, arbitration, judicial settlement, resort to regional agencies or arrangements, and other peaceful means.

**Enforcement:** A force acting under authority of the Security Council is expected to restore international peace and security by combat operations against a uniquely identified aggressor. There is no requirement for impartiality or consent; therefore, enforcement falls outside the definition of *peace operations.*

---

[2]Not only the United States but virtually all sovereign states maintain an inviolate chain of command. Note that the term *command* is often used loosely. For example, the U.N. traditionally uses the term *Force Commander*, but this officer does not command forces (except his own national contingent); he only controls them. Indeed, a Force Commander usually has weak control over forces, much weaker than operational control in U.S. practice.

**Great power:** State with influence beyond its region through some combination of wealth, military power, and traditional leadership.

**Impartiality:** Refusal to take sides in a conflict, based on the judgment that the parties share responsibility. In the context of a peace operation, *impartiality* implies that the Security Council does not intend to attain the aims of one party, or group of parties, to the exclusion of others' aims. *It does not imply that every action taken by the Security Council or states acting on its behalf will be **neutral**,* i.e., will affect all parties equally or in the same way.[3]

**Joint:** Inclusion of two or more services, e.g., U.S. Army and U.S. Marine Corps. (American military usage)

**Mandate:** Formal expression of the purpose and scope of an operation. A mandate may be expressed through Security Council resolutions, peace plans, agreements among parties, and mission statements by powers acting under authority of the Security Council.

**Non-governmental organization:** An organization that is independent of state authority and recognized by the Economic and Social Council of the United Nations as having experience or technical knowledge of value to the Council's work. (United Nations usage)

**Operational control:** "Authority to perform those functions of command over subordinate forces involving organizing and employing commands and forces, assigning tasks, designating objectives, and giving authoritative direction necessary to accomplish the mission." (Joint Chiefs of Staff, 1986, p. 3-15) "Operational control is a subset of command. It is given for a specific time frame or mission and includes the authority to assign tasks to U.S. forces already deployed by the President, and assign tasks to U.S. troops led by U.S. officers. Within the limits of operational control, a foreign UN commander *cannot*: change the mission or deploy U.S. forces outside the area of

---

[3]It is unlikely that any action, even just observing and reporting on behavior, could affect all parties equally or in the same way. The Security Council remains impartial, even when it enforces its will against a recalcitrant party, so long as this enforcement is intended to facilitate a resolution accommodating all parties. Parties do not have this Olympian perspective and usually perceive the Security Council as acting in a partisan fashion, i.e., in a manner that favors their opponents.

responsibility agreed to by the President,[4] separate units, divide their supplies, administer discipline, promote anyone, or change their internal organization." (U.S. Department of State, 1994, p. 10)

**Party:** An entity held to share responsibility for a conflict, e.g., the self-declared "Republic of Serbian Krajina" in 1991. Historically, the Security Council has recognized as "parties" rival clan leaders, representatives of ethnic communities, commanders of military formations, self-declared governments, and sovereign states.

**Peace enforcement:** A type of peace operation in which the peace force is expected to coerce recalcitrant parties into complying with their agreements or with resolutions of the Security Council.

**Peace force:** Military component of a peace operation. This force may range from unarmed observers to a joint and combined task force capable of sustained, large-scale combat.

**Peace-keeping:** (1) "Deployment of a United Nations presence in the field, hitherto with the consent of all the parties concerned, normally involving United Nations military and/or police personnel, and frequently civilians as well. Peace-keeping is a technique that expands the possibilities for both the prevention of conflict and the making of peace." (Boutros-Ghali, 1995) (2) "As the United Nations practice has evolved over the years, a peace-keeping operation has come to be defined as an operation involving military personnel, but without enforcement powers, undertaken by the United Nations to help maintain or restore international peace and security in areas of conflict. These operations are voluntary and are based on consent and co-operation. While they involve the use of military personnel, they achieve their objectives not by force of arms, thus contrasting them with the 'enforcement action' of the United Nations under Article 42. Peace-keeping operations have been most commonly employed to supervise and help maintain cease-fires, to assist in troop withdrawals, and to provide a buffer between opposing forces." (United Nations, *Blue Helmets*, 1990, pp. 4–5) (3) Obser-

---

[4]An *area of responsibility* might be some part of the entire area encompassed by the mandate. If so, disallowing the authority to order deployment outside the area of responsibility can be a significant limitation on the Force Commander. For example, the UNOSOM II commander could not order national contingents to deploy outside their assigned regions in Somalia without approval from home governments.

vation or interposition with consent of the parties. (This study; derived from cases)

**Peace operation:** Use of force to allay conflict based on initial consent of the parties and impartiality toward them. However, parties may vanish, leaving a sole legitimate government as the source of consent, e.g., western New Guinea, Haiti.

**Permanent Five:** The five powers listed in Article 23 of the Charter of the United Nations, i.e., Republic of China, France, Union of Soviet Socialist Republics (Russia), United Kingdom of Great Britain and Northern Ireland, and the United States of America. These are the prominent members of the winning coalition of World War II.

**Regional power:** State below great-power status having inherent ability to affect the outcome of a nearby conflict.

**Rules of engagement:** Directives concerning the use of lethal force, normally promulgated by the senior commander in an area of operations. Rules of engagement implement the general guidance implied by a mandate, including the invocation of Chapter VI or Chapter VII.

## *AGENDA FOR PEACE*

This appendix provides a précis and brief analysis of a typology provided by the Secretary-General of the United Nations. The Secretary-General characterizes peace operations as, among other things, keeping, making, building, or enforcing peace.

## PRÉCIS

In June 1992, Secretary-General Boutros Boutros-Ghali provided to the Security Council an "analysis and recommendations on ways of strengthening and making more efficient within the framework and provisions of the Charter the capacity of the United Nations for preventive diplomacy, for peacemaking and for peace-keeping."[1] In this report, he defines peace operations as follows:

*"Preventive diplomacy* is action to prevent disputes from arising between parties, to prevent existing disputes from escalating into conflicts and to limit the spread of the latter when they occur."[2] As examples, the Secretary-General outlines measures for confidence-building, fact-finding, early warning, preventive deployment, and establishment of demilitarized zones.[3] He broadly defines *preventive deployment* as deploying U.N. forces along international borders or

---

[1]United Nations, *Preventive Diplomacy, Peacemaking and Peace-Keeping: Report of the Secretary-General Pursuant to the Statement Adopted by the Summit Meeting of the Security Council on 31 January 1992*, A/47/277, S/24111, New York, June 17, 1992; hereafter *Agenda for Peace—1992.*

[2]United Nations, *Agenda for Peace—1992*, 1992, Paragraph 20.

[3]United Nations, *Agenda for Peace—1992*, 1992, Paragraph 23.

within a country in crisis.  "In conditions of crisis within a country, when the Government requests or all parties consent, preventive deployment could help in a number of ways to alleviate suffering and to limit or control violence."[4]

*"Peacemaking* is action to bring hostile parties to agreement, essentially through peaceful means as those foreseen in Chapter VI of the Charter of the United Nations."[5]  The expression "essentially through peaceful means" implies that the Security Council might use warlike means to make peace.  After reviewing peaceful means under Chapter VI, Boutros-Ghali reviews the possibility of coercive measures under Chapter VII.  He observes that "the Security Council has not so far made use of the most coercive of these measures—the action by military force foreseen in Article 42."[6]  Indeed, he believes that forces available to the U.N. "may perhaps never be large or well enough equipped to deal with a threat from a major army equipped with sophisticated weapons."[7]  But he recommends that the Security Council consider using "*peace enforcement units*" that would be on call and more heavily armed than peace-keeping forces.  He foresees that "peace enforcement units" might be used to "restore and maintain the cease-fire."[8]

*"Peace-keeping* is the deployment of a United Nations presence in the field, hitherto with the consent[9] of all the parties concerned, normally involving United Nations military and/or police personnel

---

[4]United Nations, *Agenda for Peace—1992,* 1992, Paragraph 29. The phrase "all parties consent" implies that the Secretary-General envisions factions competing for control over a country.  The words *suffering* and *violence* suggest that the crisis must be verging on conflict.  Such circumstances make the expression *"preventive* deployment" seem oddly chosen, but the Secretary-General evidently means that the peace force could prevent the conflict from worsening or spreading.

[5]United Nations, *Agenda for Peace—1992,* 1992, Paragraph 20.

[6]United Nations, *Agenda for Peace—1992,* 1992, Paragraph 42. This statement covers all cases, including Korea and Kuwait, because these enforcement actions were carried out by member states acting *under authority of* the U.N., not *by* the U.N.

[7]United Nations, *Agenda for Peace—1992,* 1992, Paragraph 43.

[8]United Nations, *Agenda for Peace—1992,* 1992, Paragraph 44.

[9]The expression "hitherto with consent" muddies the definition because it implies that the Security Council might undertake "peace-keeping" without consent. But if it were undertaken without consent during an ongoing conflict, what would distinguish "peace-keeping" from "peace enforcement"?

and frequently civilians as well. Peace-keeping is a technique that expands the possibilities for both the prevention of conflict and the making of peace."[10] Boutros-Ghali considers "peace-keeping" an invention of the U.N. that has evolved rapidly in recent years and may not have precise boundaries: "Just as diplomacy will continue across the span of all the activities dealt with in the present report, so there may not be a dividing line between peacemaking and peace-keeping."[11]

"... *peace-building*—action to identify and support structures which will tend to strengthen and solidify peace in order to avoid a relapse into conflict."[12]

## ANALYSIS

Figure B.1 presents a schematic overview of the typology contained in *Agenda for Peace—1992.*

The typology contained in *Agenda for Peace* is difficult to apply because it defines operations by progress toward "peace," an ambiguously defined concept. Does "peace" imply absence of armed conflict among states or other parties? Or does it imply an acceptable degree of civil order? In a recent example, Krajina Serbs conducted "ethnic cleansing" while fitfully observing a fragile cease-fire. Was there "peace" or not? Would "peace" imply fewer cease-fire violations, or fewer persons driven from their homes, or some mixture of both?

However "peace" were defined, it would be infinitely variable and subject to sudden changes, making a typology based on "peace" of doubtful practicality. Even among states, "peace" is highly variable. To what extent are Israel and Syria, or India and Pakistan, currently at "peace"?

Variability becomes much greater for protracted conflict between factions within a state, such as Somalia during 1992–1995. During

---

[10]United Nations, *Agenda for Peace—1992,* 1992, Paragraph 20.

[11]United Nations, *Agenda for Peace—1992,* 1992, Paragraph 45.

[12]United Nations, *Agenda for Peace—1992,* 1992, Paragraph 21.

RAND*MR583-B.1*

| | Preventive Deployment | Peace-Keeping[a] | Peacemaking[a] | | Peace-Building |
| | | | Peacemaking (peaceful means) | Peace Enforcement | |
|---|---|---|---|---|---|
| Chapter of the U.N. Charter | Chapter VI | Chapter VI (also Chapter VII?) | Chapter VI | Article 40, Chapter VII | Chapter VI |
| Consent Required from the Parties | Request of Government or all parties or with their consent (Paragraph 28) | "Hitherto with consent" (Paragraph 20) Cooperate in implementing mandate (Paragraph 50) | "Seek a solution" to differences (Paragraph 34) | | Cooperate in "construction of a new environment" (Paragraph 57) |
| Typical Mandate | Deploy on both sides or one side of border; provide humanitarian aid; maintain security (Paragraphs 28, 29) | Provide presence to prevent conflict or to make peace (Paragraph 20) | Bring hostile parties to agreement essentially through peaceful means (Paragraph 20) | "Respond to outright aggression, imminent or actual" (Paragraph 44) | Disarm parties; restore order; repatriate refugees; train security personnel; monitor elections; protect human rights; reform governmental institutions (Paragraph 55) |

[a] "... there may not be a dividing line between peacemaking and peace-keeping. Peacemaking is often a prelude to peace-keeping." (United Nations, *Agenda for Peace—1992*, 1992, Paragraph 45)

**Figure B.1—Typology of Peace Operations in *Agenda for Peace—1992***

those years, much of Somalia was peaceful, although parts of the country were plagued by violent power struggles and sheer banditry. During roughly the same period, Bosnia-Herzegovina presented an even more complicated picture of civil conflict overlaid with conflict among states, interrupted by numerous cease-fires, and influenced by informal local agreements. A typology of peace operations that depends on the condition of "peace" would imply bewildering shifts among peace-keeping, peacemaking, and peace-building as the condition of "peace" changed.

Compounding these difficulties, *Agenda for Peace—1992* allows types of operations to overlap in a confusing way. "Peace-keeping" is not clearly differentiated from "peacemaking" nor given any definite content. "Peace-making" includes radically dissimilar operations, ranging from traditional peace-keeping through peace enforcement under Chapter VII. This exceptionally wide definition is confusing and unhelpful.

Buried within *Agenda for Peace—1992* is an urgent warning to the Security Council concerning the safety of U.N. personnel:

> Given the pressing need to afford adequate protection to United Nations personnel engaged in life-endangering circumstances, I recommend that the Security Council, unless it elects immediately to withdraw the United Nations personnel in order to preserve the credibility of the Organization, gravely consider what action should be taken towards those who put United Nations personnel in danger.[13]

Boutros-Ghali suggests that, before deployment occurs, the Council should consider what actions it will take, including those under Chapter VII, if parties frustrate the operation and hostilities occur. Subsequent events in Somalia and Bosnia-Herzegovina gave this warning a prophetic ring.

In January 1995, Boutros-Ghali revisited *Agenda for Peace—1992*. In addition to the typology offered previously, he identified a "new type of United Nations operation":

> This [reference to humanitarian aid] has led in Bosnia and Herzegovina and in Somalia to a new type of United Nations operation. Even though the use of force is authorized under Chapter VII of the Charter, the United Nations remains neutral and impartial between the warring parties, without a mandate to stop the aggressor (if one can be identified)[14] or impose a cessation of hostilities. Nor is this peace-keeping as practiced hitherto, because the hostilities continue and there is often no agreement between the warring parties on which a peace mandate can be based. The "safe areas" concept in Bosnia and Herzegovina is a similar case.[15]

---

[13]United Nations, *Agenda for Peace—1992,* 1992, Paragraph 67.

[14]This formulation confuses an important issue. Of course, the Council might identify an aggressor, deplore its aggression, and decline to take action. But would it be politically feasible or morally defensible for the Council to identify an aggressor and take actions designed to preserve impartiality between it and its victims? Almost certainly not, and therefore Boutros-Ghali should have offered a clear dichotomy: either the Council has decided to be impartial among warring parties or it has identified an aggressor and therefore is not impartial.

[15]United Nations, *Supplement to An Agenda for Peace: Position Paper of the Secretary-General on the Occasion of the Fiftieth Anniversary of the United Nations,* A/50/60, S/1995/1, New York, January 3, 1995, Paragraph 19; hereafter, *Agenda for Peace—1995.*

The statement that the U.N. "remains neutral and impartial" raises difficulties. Was it neutral to authorize the arrest of Mohammed Farah Aideed in Somalia? To defend Muslim-populated safe areas against Serb attacks using NATO air power? These actions were *impartial* in that they were not intended to attain the overall political goals of any party to the conflict, but they were certainly not *neutral*, in the sense of affecting all parties equally. On the contrary, they were largely or exclusively directed against certain parties considered obstructive to the peace process.

Boutros-Ghali assessed the causes of failure in Somalia and Bosnia-Herzegovina as follows:

> In reality, nothing is more dangerous for a peace-keeping operation than to ask it to use force when its existing composition, armament, logistic support and deployment deny it the capability to do so. The logic of peace-keeping flows from political and military premises that are quite distinct from those of enforcement; and the dynamics of the latter are incompatible with the political process that peace-keeping is intended to facilitate. To blur the distinction between the two can undermine the viability of the peace-keeping operation and endanger its personnel.[16]

The Secretary-General correctly argued that failure had two causes: (1) changing to peace enforcement mandates without providing the required forces and (2) attempting to combine incompatible types of operations, i.e., traditional peace-keeping and peace enforcement. He might have added that viable agreements among the parties are prerequisites for all peace operations based on continuous consent. In the absence of viable agreements, peace-keeping is ineffective and dangerous to the peace force—especially in Bosnia-Herzegovina. There, the Security Council mounted traditional peace-keeping operations to implement agreements that were ephemeral and usually *male fide*; therefore, those operations were ill-conceived and were failing even before the Security Council made half-hearted attempts at peace enforcement.

---

[16]United Nations, *Agenda for Peace—1995*, 1995, Paragraph 35.

# STANDARDS FOR U.S. INVOLVEMENT

In early 1994, the Clinton Administration announced a policy to reform multilateral peace operations. Outlined in *The Clinton Administration's Policy on Reforming Multilateral Peace Operations* (U.S. Department of State, 1994), this policy includes shared responsibility between the Department of State and the Department of Defense, increased consultation with Congress, and initiatives to strengthen the United Nations as an organization.

At the heart of this policy are three standards for American involvement in peace operations. The standards are intended to guide decisionmakers in making disciplined, coherent choices about support for peace operations. They include criteria for an affirmative vote in the Security Council, for the participation of American personnel when combat is not anticipated, and for the participation of American personnel in operations that are likely to involve combat. Details of the three standards are presented in the following sections.

## STANDARD ONE—U.S. CASTS AFFIRMATIVE VOTE:

- U.N. involvement advances U.S. interests, and there is an international community of interest for dealing with the problem multilaterally.

- There is a threat to or breach of international peace and security, often of a regional character, defined as one or a combination of the following:

- — International aggression
- — Urgent humanitarian disaster coupled with violence
- — Sudden interruption of established democracy or gross violation of human rights, coupled with violence or threat of violence.

- There are clear objectives and an understanding of where the mission fits on the spectrum between traditional peace-keeping and peace enforcement.

- For traditional (Chapter VI) peace-keeping operations, a cease-fire should be in place and the consent of the parties should be obtained before the force is deployed.

- For peace enforcement (Chapter VII) operations, the threat to international peace and security should be considered significant.

- The means to accomplish the mission are available, including the force, financing, and a mandate appropriate to the mission.

- The political, economic, and humanitarian consequences of inaction by the international community have been weighed and are considered unacceptable.

- The operation's anticipated duration is tied to clear objectives and realistic criteria for ending the operation.

## STANDARD TWO—U.S. PERSONNEL PARTICIPATE AND COMBAT IS UNLIKELY:

- Participation advances U.S. interests, and both the unique and general risks to American personnel have been weighed and are considered acceptable.

- Personnel, funds, and other resources are available.

- U.S. participation is necessary for the operation's success.

- The role of U.S. forces is tied to clear objectives, and an endpoint for U.S. participation can be identified.

- Domestic and congressional support exists or can be marshaled.

- Command-and-control arrangements are acceptable.

## STANDARD THREE—U.S. PERSONNEL PARTICIPATE AND COMBAT IS LIKELY:

- There exists a determination to commit sufficient forces to achieve clearly defined objectives.

- There exists a plan to achieve those objectives decisively.

- There exists a commitment to reassess and adjust, as necessary, the size, composition, and disposition of U.S. forces to achieve U.S. objectives.

# SELECT BIBLIOGRAPHY

Alberts, David S., and Richard Hayes, *Command Arrangements for Peace Operations*, National Defense University Press, Washington, D.C., 1995.

Albright, Madeleine, "The Myths About UN Peace-Keeping," *Statement to the House Foreign Affairs Subcommittee on International Security, International Organizations, and Human Rights*, Washington, D.C., June 24, 1993.

Allard, Kenneth, *Somalia Operations: Lessons Learned*, National Defense University Press, Washington, D.C., 1995.

Allen, William W., Antione D. Johnson, and John T. Nelsen II, "Peace-Keeping and Peace Enforcement Operations," *Military Review*, October 1993, pp. 53–61.

Armstrong, Charles L., "From Futility to Insanity: A Brief Review of UN Failures," *Military Technology*, December 1994, pp. 89–91.

Baehr, Peter R., and Leon Gordenker, *The United Nations in the 1990s*, St. Martin's Press, New York, 1992.

Berkowitz, Bruce D., "Rules of Engagement for UN Peace-Keeping Forces in Bosnia," *Orbis*, Fall 1994, pp. 635–646.

Betts, Richard K., "The Delusion of Impartial Intervention," *Foreign Affairs*, November/December 1994, pp. 20–33.

Blechman, Barry M., and J. Matthew Vaccaro, *Training for Peace-Keeping: The United Nations' Role,* The Henry L. Stimson Center, Washington, D.C., Report No. 12, July 1994.

Boutros-Ghali, Boutros, *An Agenda for Peace: 1995,* United Nations, New York, 1995.

Branaman, Brenda M., *Somalia: Chronology of Events, June 26, 1960—October 14, 1993,* Congressional Research Service, Washington, D.C., October 15, 1993.

Brooks, Geraldine, "Peace-Keeping Missions of UN Are Pursued on a Wing and a Prayer," *Wall Street Journal,* December 28, 1993, p. 1.

Browne, Marjorie Ann, *United Nations Peace-Keeping: Historical Overview,* Congressional Research Service, Washington, D.C., CRS Report 90-96F, January 31, 1990.

———, *United Nations Peace-Keeping Operations 1988–1993: Background Information,* Congressional Research Service, Washington, D.C., CRS Report 94-193F, February 28, 1994.

Bruner, Edward F., *U.S. Forces and Multinational Commands: Precedents and Criteria,* Congressional Research Service, Washington, D.C., CRS Report 93-436F, April 21, 1993.

Cassesse, Antonio, ed., *United Nations Peace-Keeping: Legal Essays,* Sijthoff and Noordhoff, Netherlands, 1978.

Chairman, Joint Chiefs of Staff, *Department of Defense Dictionary of Military and Associated Terms,* Washington, D.C., CJCS, Joint Publication 1-02, March 23, 1994.

Chayes, Antonia Handler, and George T. Raach, eds., *Peace Operations: Developing an American Strategy,"* National Defense University Press, Washington, D.C., 1995.

Copson, Raymond W., *Somalia: Operation Restore Hope,* Congressional Research Service, Washington, D.C., April 6, 1993.

Crocker, Chester A., "Peace-Keeping We Can Fight For," *The Washington Post,* May 8, 1994, p. C1.

Dagne, Theodros S., *Somalia: A Country at War—Prospects for Peace and Reconciliation*, Congressional Research Service, Washington, D.C., June 15, 1992.

Diehl, Paul F., "Peace-Keeping Operations and the Quest for Peace," *Political Science Quarterly*, Vol. 103, No. 3, 1988, pp. 485–507.

Durch, William J., ed., *The Evolution of UN Peacekeeping: Case Studies and Comparative Analysis*, 2nd ed., St. Martin's Press, New York, 1993.

Dworken, Jonathan T., *Military Relations with Humanitarian Relief Organizations: Observations from Restore Hope*, Center for Naval Analyses, Alexandria, Va., CRM-94-140, October 1993.

Elganzoury, Abdelazim, *Evolution of the Peace Keeping Powers of the General Assembly of the United Nations*, General Egyptian Book Organization, Cairo, 1978.

Foss, John, et al., "U.S. Forces on the Golan Heights?" Center for Security Policy, Washington, D.C., October 25, 1994; reprinted in *Commentary*, December 1994.

Freeman, Waldo D., Robert B. Lambert, and Jason D. Mims, "Operation Restore Hope: A USCENTCOM Perspective," *Military Review*, September 1993.

Garvey, Jack, "United Nations Peace-Keeping and Host State Consent," *American Journal of International Law*, April 1970, pp. 241–269.

Gellman, Barton, "Somalia Options Reviewed as Discontent in Congress Grows," *Washington Post*, October 6, 1993, pp. A1, A12.

Glenny, Misja, *The Fall of Yugoslavia: The Third Balkan War*, Penguin Books, New York, 1992.

Gonin, Jean-Marc, "ONU: Les Gardiens de la Paix," *L'Express*, April 15, 1993, pp. 20–25.

Gordenker, Leon, *Soldiers, Peacekeepers and Disasters*, St. Martin's Press, New York, 1991.

Herzog, Chaim, *The Arab-Israeli Wars*, Random House, New York, 1982.

Hoar, Joseph P., "A CINC's Perspective," *JFQ Forum*, Autumn 1993.

Joint Chiefs of Staff, *Unified Action Armed Forces (UNAAF)*, Washington, D.C., JCS Publication 0-2, December 1, 1986.

Kanter, Arnold, "Intervention Decision-Making During the Bush Administration:  Deciding Where to Go In and When to Get Out," *Special Warfare*, April 1995, pp. 14–23.

Kassebaum, Nancy L., and Lee H. Hamilton, *Peace-Keeping and the U.S. National Interest*, The Henry L. Stimson Center, Washington, D.C., Report No. 11, February 1994.

Kassing, David, *Transporting the Army for Operation Restore Hope*, RAND, Santa Monica, Calif., MR-384-A, 1994.

Lake, Anthony, "The Limits of Peace-Keeping," *The New York Times*, February 6, 1994, p. D17.

Leibstone, Marvin, "Peace-Keeping '94:  More Questions Than Answers," *Military Technology*, December 1994, pp. 84–85.

Lippman, Thomas W., "Use of U.S. Troops on Golan Heights Debated," *Washington Post*, December 4, 1994, p. 42.

Lowenthal, Mark M., *Peace-Keeping in Future U.S. Foreign Policy: CRS Report to Congress*, Congressional Reporting Service, Washington, D.C., March 21, 1994, pp. 1–22.

MacKenzie, Lewis, *Peacekeeper: The Road to Sarajevo*, Douglas & McIntyre, Vancouver, Canada, 1993.

Mann, Edward, "Military Support for 'Peace Efforts'," *Airpower Journal*, Fall 1993, pp. 51–56.

Merryman, James L., "New World Order Is Tested by Somalia," *The Christian Science Monitor*, February 1, 1995.

Mousavizadeh, Nader, ed., *The Black Book of Bosnia*, BasicBooks, New York, 1996.

Nelson, Richard, "Multinational Peace-Keeping in the Middle East and the United Nations Model," *International Affairs*, Winter 1984–85, pp. 67–89.

Niblack, Preston, Thomas S. Szayna, and John Bordeaux, *Increasing the Availability and Effectiveness of Non–U.S. Forces for Peace Operations*, RAND, Santa Monica, Calif., MR-701-OSD, 1996.

Palin, Roger H., *Multinational Military Forces: Problems and Prospects*, Oxford University Press, London, Adelphi Paper 294, 1995.

Powell, Colin, *My American Journey*, Random House, New York, 1995.

Rifkind, Malcolm, "Peace-Keeping or Peacemaking? Implications and Prospects," *RUSI Journal*, April 1993, pp. 1–6.

Rikhye, Indar Jit, Michael Harbottle, and Bjorn Egge, *The Thin Blue Line: International Peace-Keeping and Its Future*, Yale University Press, New Haven, Conn., 1974.

Roberts, Adam, "The Crisis in UN Peace-Keeping," *Survival: The IISS Quarterly*, Autumn 1994, pp. 93–120.

Roos, John G., "The Perils of Peace-Keeping: Tallying the Costs in Blood, Coin, Prestige, and Readiness," *Armed Forces Journal International*, December 1993, pp. 13–17.

Saksena, K. P., "Not by Design: Evolution of UN Peace-Keeping Operations and Its Implications for the Future," *International Studies*, October–December 1977, pp. 459–481.

Sherry, George L., *The United Nations: Conflict Control in the Post–Cold War World*, Council on Foreign Relations, New York, 1990.

Siegel, Adam B., *Requirements for Humanitarian Assistance and Peace Operations: Insights from Seven Case Studies*, Center for Naval Analyses, Alexandria, Va., CRM-94-74, March 1995.

Sloan, Stanley R., *Peace-Keeping and Conflict Management Activities: A Discussion of Terms*, Congressional Research Service, Washington, D.C., CRS Report 93-1017S, November 26, 1993.

Stewart, Bob, *Broken Lives: A Personal View of the Bosnian Conflict,* HarperCollins, London, 1993.

Swift, Richard, "United Nations Military Training for Peace," *International Organization,* Spring 1974, pp. 267–280.

Tharoor, Shashi, "Peace-Keeping:  Principles, Problems, Prospects," *Naval War College Review,* Spring 1994, pp. 9–22.

United Nations, *The Blue Helmets: A Review of United Nations Peace-Keeping,* 2nd ed., Department of Public Information, New York, 1990.

——, *Charter of the United Nations,* San Francisco Calif., June 25, 1945.

——, *Preventive Diplomacy, Peacemaking and Peace-Keeping: Report of the Secretary-General Pursuant to the Statement Adopted by the Summit Meeting of the Security Council on 31 January 1992,* A/47/277, S/24111, New York, June 17, 1992; short title: *Agenda for Peace—1992.*

——, *Supplement to An Agenda for Peace:  Position Paper of the Secretary-General on the Occasion of the Fiftieth Anniversary of the United Nations,* A/50/60–S/1995/1, New York, January 3, 1995.

——, *The United Nations and Cambodia 1991–1995,* Department of Public Information, New York, 1995.

——, *The United Nations and Mozambique 1992–1995,* Department of Public Information, New York, 1995.

——, *United Nations Peace-Keeping,* Department of Public Information, New York, August 1993.

——, *Universal Declaration of Human Rights,* adopted by General Assembly on December 10, 1948.

"United Nations Peace-Keeping Operations:  History, Resources, Missions, and Components," *International Defense Review: Defense 1995,* 1995, pp. 119–127.

U.S. Department of the Army, Center for Lessons Learned, U.S. Army Combined Arms Command, *Operation Restore Hope: Operations Other Than War,* Fort Leavenworth, Kansas, August 16, 1993.

——, Headquarters, 1st Brigade, 10th Mountain Division (Light Infantry), *After Action Report: Task Force Mountain Warrior,* Fort Drum, New York, September 30, 1993.

——, 10th Mountain Division (LI), U.S. Army Forces, *Somalia: After Action Report,* Fort Drum, New York, June 2, 1993.

U.S. Department of State, *The Clinton Administration's Policy on Reforming Multilateral Peace Operations,* Washington, D.C., Publication 10161, May 1994.

U.S. General Accounting Office, National Security and International Affairs Division, *Humanitarian Intervention: Effectiveness of UN Operations in Bosnia,* Washington, D.C., GAO/NSIAD-94-156BR, April 1994.

——, *UN Peacekeeping: Lessons Learned in Managing Recent Missions,* Washington, D.C., GAO/NSIAD-94-9, December 1993.

——, *United Nations: U.S. Participation in Peace-Keeping Operations,* Washington, D.C., GAO/NSIAD-92-247, September 1992.

U.S. Government, *A National Security Strategy of Engagement and Enlargement,* The White House, Washington, D.C., July 1994.

U.S. Institute of Peace, *Contributions to the Study of Peacemaking, Volume 3,* Washington, D.C., 1993.

van Heuven, Marten, "Rehabilitating Serbia," *Foreign Policy,* Fall 1994, pp. 38–56.

von Koispoth, Edward, "Airborne Surveillance for UN Crisis Management," *Military Technology,* December 1994, pp. 87–88.

Ward, Don, "Getting a Handle on Peace-Keeping," *Navy Times,* March 14, 1994, p. 29.

Warrington, Robert D., "The Helmets May Be Blue, but the Blood's Still Red: The Dilemma of U.S. Participation in UN Peace Operations," *Comparative Strategy,* Vol. 14, No. 1, 1995, pp. 23–34.

Woodward, Susan L., *Balkan Tragedy:  Chaos and Dissolution After the Cold War*, The Brookings Institution, Washington, D.C., 1995.

Zimmerman, Warren, "The Last Ambassador:  A Memoir of the Collapse of Yugoslavia," *Foreign Affairs*, March/April 1995, pp. 2–20.